OTTAWA AUG. 2003

# Jean Paul LEMIEUX

His…

CW01619058

# Jean Paul

# LEMIEUX

## His Canada

Canadian Postal Museum

Canadian Museum of Civilization

Canadian Cataloguing in Publication Data

Brousseau, Francine

Jean Paul Lemieux: his Canada

Exhibition catalogue.
Issued also in French under title: Jean Paul Lemieux, visions du Canada.

Issued by the Canadian Museum of Civilization.
ISBN 0-660-10797-X

1. Lemieux, Jean-Paul, 1904–1990 – Exhibitions.
2. Canadian Postal Museum – Exhibitions.
I. Canadian Postal Museum.
II. Canadian Museum of Civilization.
III. Title.

ND249.L4B76 1998 759.11 C98-980024-5

This publication was produced by the Canadian Postal Museum in association with the National Archives of Canada and is sponsored by Pitney Bowes.

Research: Sylvia Antoniou and Francine Brousseau
Design: Triad Design Inc.
Photographs of the series His Canada: Harry Foster, Canadian Museum of Civilization

Sincere thanks to:
Yousuf Karsh
Canada Post Corporation
National Archives of Canada
Pitney Bowes

Printed in Canada

Cover: *Saskatchewan* (detail)

# *Contents*

# *Foreword*

The Canadian Postal Museum takes great pride in presenting *Jean Paul Lemieux: His Canada,* an exhibition that includes twelve outstanding works by this great Canadian painter.

As curator of the Museum's art collection, I had studied the paintings in the *His Canada* series when the exhibition initially opened in 1984 at the National Postal Museum. I had also written the text of a catalogue, which we are now publishing here for the first time complete with an updated biography of the artist.

The catalogue also contains a number of quotations by Lemieux, as well as some explanations about the paintings in the *His Canada* series. Extracted from an interview with the artist that was done at the time by the National Postal Museum but never published, this material is all the more interesting today.

Since the 1950s, thousands of works of art have been created to illustrate postage stamps. These constitute a unique store of images of Canada's artistic and natural heritage, its history and people. We are pleased to share this unique collection preserved at the National Archives of Canada, and to allow you to discover the varied aspects of our great country.

I would like to express my gratitude to the National Archives of Canada, our partner in producing the exhibition and catalogue. A very special and sincere thank you as well goes to Pitney Bowes for its support of all the activities of the Pitney Bowes Art Gallery at the Canadian Postal Museum.

Francine Brousseau
Exhibition Curator
Director, Canadian Postal Museum

*We must achieve silence within ourselves, a silence of that profound sort which alone enables us to hear the prodigious silence of the universe, the austere and splendid silence of Lemieux. What lurks here is not just silence but the invisible, challenging us to capture it, as we are invited to this contemplation, to this beyond. No point in trying to dodge this pressing invitation, this summons out of time. Why attempt to flee, like certain characters from the paintings, right at the edge of the frame? Are we that attached to life as we know it?*

Anne Hébert

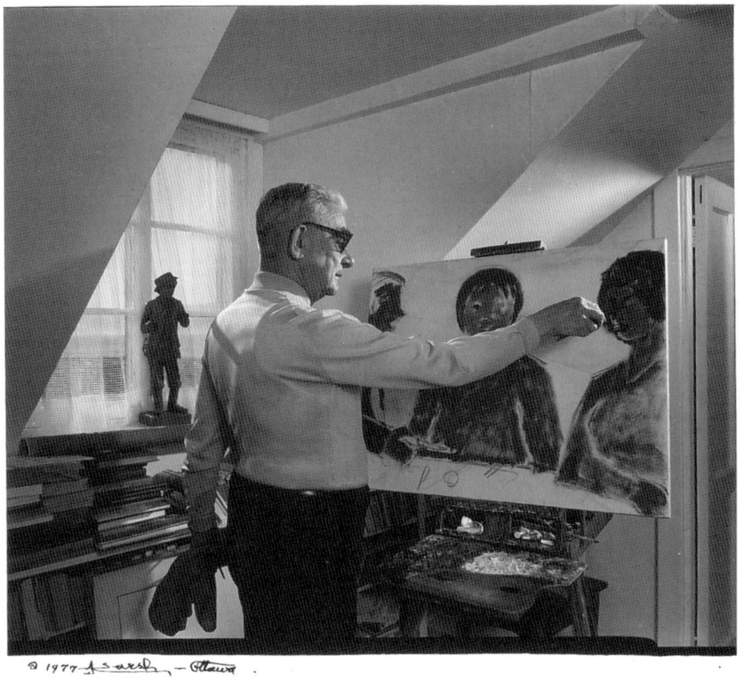

*Jean Paul Lemieux,* 1979
Photograph by Yousuf Karsh

# *Art and the post*

In *Jean Paul Lemieux: His Canada,* the Canadian Postal Museum presents twelve paintings by Lemieux that constitute a new aspect of the work of this great Canadian painter. He created this series of small-scale canvases expressly for printing as a block of commemorative stamps for Canada Day 1984.

Since the 1950s, Canada Post has invited artists to create new works or has chosen works from Canadian museums or private collections to illustrate its postage stamps. All of the images submitted for consideration, as well as those eventually used for reproduction on postage stamps, are kept in the National Archives of Canada.

This collection of art is unique and bears little resemblance to the collections of other museums. The works reveal the artists in a different light: each work having been commissioned, the subject matter is predetermined and does not necessarily reflect the artist's own inclinations. Working on a reduced scale, the artist must bear in mind that the composition will be miniaturized and reproduced millions of times over, to be seen by millions of people.

# Biography

Jean Paul Lemieux was born in Quebec City on November 18, 1904. His childhood years were divided between Quebec City and Kent House, a hotel situated above Montmorency Falls, where the family took up residence from May to November. It was there he met the American artist Charles Parnell, who painted decorative murals for the hotel. In 1917, after a year in California, the family settled in Montreal, spending their summers in the Charlevoix region. Lemieux studied at Mont Saint-Louis, at Loyola College, and took watercolour classes.

By the time he entered Montreal's École des beaux-arts in 1926, Lemieux had already filled several sketchbooks and even produced a first oil painting, *Montmorency Falls* (1923). He also studied with Marc-Aurèle de Foy Suzor-Coté and Edwin Holgate, two prominent names in Canadian painting.

Lemieux spent 1929 in Paris accompanied by his mother, where he met the Canadian painter Clarence Gagnon, attended courses at the Grande Chaumière and the Colarossi Academy, and moved in artistic circles at the height of the Surrealist movement. He was also interested in commercial art and illustration. On his return from Europe in 1930 he founded a design and illustration firm with Jori Smith and Jean Palardy, but after six fairly inconclusive months, they dissolved the partnership and Lemieux went back to California to draw and paint. Returning to the École des beaux-arts in 1931, he received his diploma in 1934 and took up a teaching position at the school. The following year he also taught at Montreal's École du meuble.

The year 1937 marked Lemieux's homecoming to Quebec City, where he accepted a teaching post at the École des beaux-arts and married Madeleine Desrosiers, an artist and classmate from Montreal's École des beaux-arts. Lemieux taught at the École des beaux-arts in Quebec City until his retirement in 1967. He continued to paint until his death in 1990, dividing his time between the city, where he spent the winter, and Île aux Coudres in Charlevoix, where he enjoyed the summer months.

Throughout his career, Lemieux wrote, lectured, taught children, and helped run artistic associations, in addition to his teaching at the École des beaux-arts. He also illustrated numerous books and painted murals and official portraits.

Jean Paul Lemieux became an associate member of the Royal Canadian Academy of Arts in 1951 and was elected a full member in 1966. He joined Quebec's Société des arts plastiques in 1956. In 1968 Lemieux was named to the Order of Canada, and in 1970 was awarded two honorary doctorates. He received yet another honorary degree in 1985. In 1990 he was nominated a member of the Académie des grands Québécois. He died on December 7, 1990. In 1997 he was posthumously made grand chevalier of the Ordre du Québec. The quality and originality of his work also earned him numerous prizes.

# What is a Lemieux?

Jean Paul Lemieux is not a painter who belongs to any school or movement, although he took an interest in a number of groups such as the Surrealists, the Group of Seven, and the Ashcan School. He always shied away from fashionable trends in order to develop a unique style, one that drew upon his own individuality and personal experience for inspiration. His entire work is based on his personal vision ... a vision of city and countryside spanning the seasons ... a vision of humanity at all stages of life.

It is difficult to divide Lemieux's work into periods. There is an early style, which stretches over some thirty years, and there is a Lemieux style, which emerged halfway through his career. Four

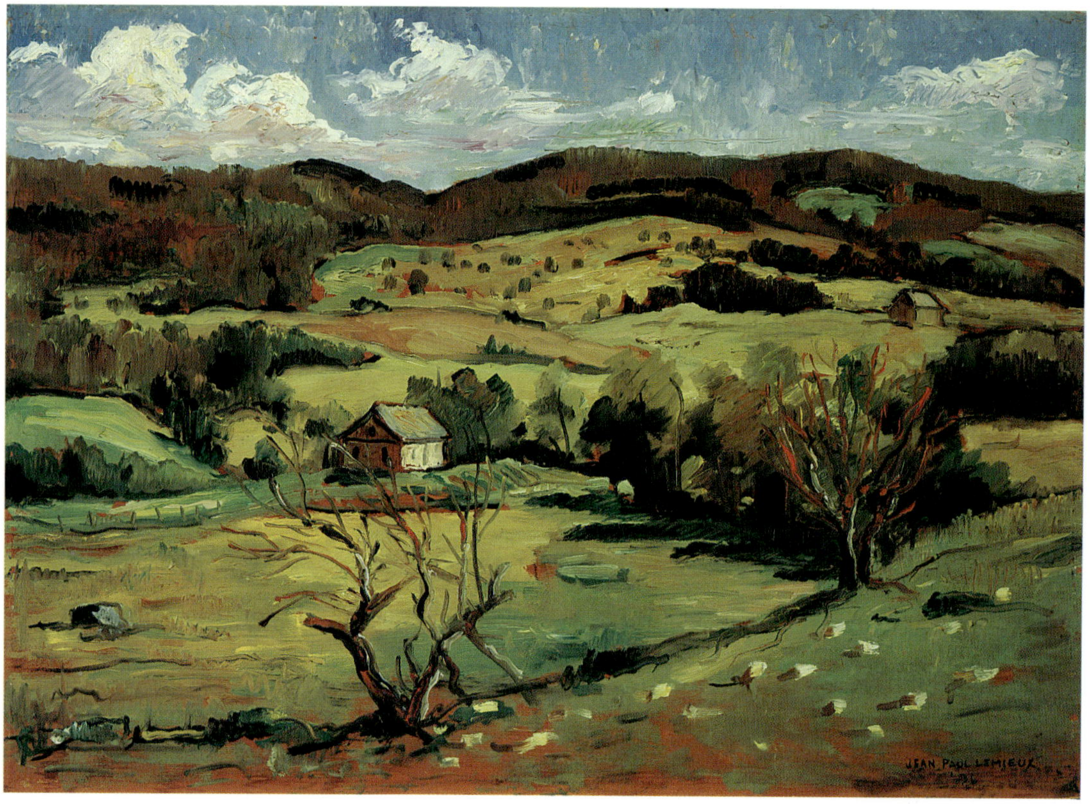

*Landscape, Eastern Townships,* 1936
Musée du Québec

*It is interpretation, personal vision, and sensibility that count in a painting. The subject is only a point of departure, a basis on which to construct an image that one uses to express one's emotion and one's soul.*

Lemieux, 1938

works from the early period are reproduced in this book; the later period is represented by the twelve paintings of *His Canada*.

Lemieux began by creating elaborate landscapes and scenes of a naive or picturesque sort, such as *Montmorency Falls, Landscape, Charlevoix* (1935), *Landscape, Eastern Townships* (1936), *Lazarus* (1941), *Fête-Dieu in Quebec City* (1944), and *The Birds I Have Known* (1947). These early paintings do not bear the stamp of the artist as we now know him; they are not readily identified today as Lemieux's. His artistic aim at that stage was shaped by a desire to reproduce reality faithfully by figurative works, and by the sense of humour that he brought to his character studies.

About 1950 Lemieux reached a turning point at which he began refining his style: details disappeared, the palette became more restricted, objects and human figures became simplified or distorted. *The Ursuline Nuns* (1951), along with the prelimimary drawings for this painting, and *Solitude* (1953) are good examples of this evolution, although a picture like *Quebec City* (1952), in the tradition of *Lazarus* and *Fête-Dieu in Quebec City*, shows that Lemieux had not completely broken with his earlier style.

In 1954 Lemieux was awarded a scholarship from the Royal Society of Canada, which allowed him to work for a year in France, specifically in Paris, the Côte d'Azur, and Brittany. Spending a year far from the places he loved best, knew well, and had painted for more than twenty-five years led to his discovery of the extent to which Canada is horizontal. To capture this quality, Lemieux's paintings would from then on be marked by a horizontal perspective, his compositions almost always sectioned off or divided by a horizon line. Several works executed in 1956 – *The Distant City, The Road That Leads Nowhere,* and *The Noon Train* – bear witness to this discovery.

The sojourn in France made the artist realize that what he felt and wished to paint stemmed from his physical surroundings, the quality of the light, and the attitudes and individuals peculiar to a country.

Because Lemieux's paintings depict a vast and often cold and barren country, his subjects developed around a sense of confrontation with wide-open spaces, cold, solitude, and isolation. Being conscious of the burden of time that affects all of us, he sets his compositions in a precise moment. These paintings aspire to being more a condition or an emotion than a mere subject or landscape. Lemieux produces works that create a kind of intimate rapport with the observer, an intimacy that is often conveyed through a human figure.

After the period 1955–56, Lemieux's figures begin to become more prominent. Often truncated and situated on the very edge of the painting, they fix us with a penetrating gaze. Even though the artist has simplified their actions and expressions, they are still striking, bearing the burden of space and time. They are as unmistakable a product of Lemieux as the earlier tilted horizons and vast, flat, uniform surfaces. *Remembered* (1962), *Death on a Clear Morning* (1963), *Julie and the Universe*, (1967), *Amelie and Time* (1965), *Orion* (1967), *Encounter* (1968), *Tribute to Nelligan* (1971), *Maria Chapdelaine,* and *François Paradis* (1981) are several of the pictures whose characters make a strong impression on the viewer.

After the 1950s Lemieux continued to explore composition and technique. Even if the arrangement of elements in a picture, as well as the forms and colours themselves, were greatly pared down over the years, this process of simplification did not steer Lemieux toward abstract art. He remains a figurative painter, albeit one who avoids complexity. Nor did Lemieux strive for technical expertise in painting his objects and human figures. He applies colours subtly, in either short or long rectangular strokes that seem to be separated from one another, and that bring to life a figurative composition.

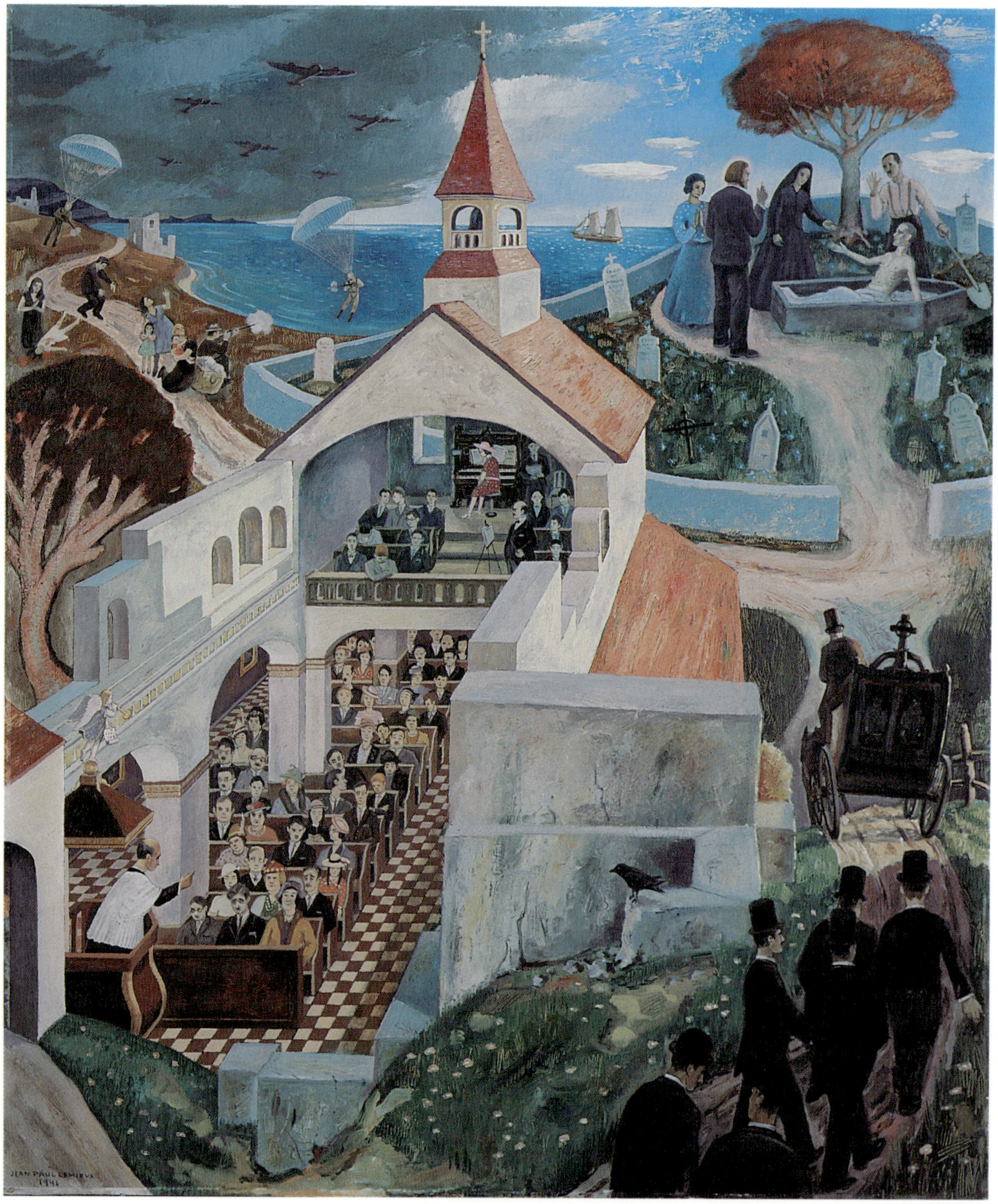


*Lazarus,* 1941
Art Gallery of Ontario

Over the years, Lemieux's touch changed somewhat; the paint is more transparent and sparse in certain places. But although his hand sometimes seems less sure, the emotion remains. All the critics agree that Lemieux's art is an art of emotion. As with Julie of the 1960s, Maria Chapdelaine, François Paradis, or the figure in *Saskatchewan* are products of the same sentiments, inviting us to share their reality.

How is it that the same pictorial organization, the same light, the same perspective, all of which show a disregard for contemporary artistic movements, have nevertheless managed to make Lemieux's work endure? Is it because of the emotion and the strange sense of complicity we feel when confronted with his images that we never tire of these paintings with all their repetitive elements? The artist speaks a language understood by all and invites us to look beyond.

We have captured the essence if we see Lemieux as a painter of wide-open spaces, fleeting moments of time, and striking characters. The variety of his subjects has continued to draw on these few constants for over half a century.

Visitors to galleries showing the work of young Quebec artists often find Lemieux-like characters staring out at them, as well as many pictures composed in the manner of a Lemieux. Yet one critic has commented: "Nobody was Lemieux's predecessor and nobody will be his heir." This introductory essay has not attempted to determine the possible antecedents of Lemieux's work or to measure the extent of his influence. Its purpose has been simply to show how the twelve paintings presented in this exhibition relate to the painter's work as a whole.

## *The His Canada Series*

*His Canada* was the title that suggested itself for these twelve images. The unveiling of the stamps and opening of the first version of the exhibition was held on June 29, 1984, in Quebec City. The Governor General of Canada, Her Excellency Madame Jeanne Sauvé, presided over the ceremony at her Citadel residence, which had so often been rendered by the artist in the past. Jean Paul Lemieux stood facing his paintings surrounded by a group of enraptured onlookers. "This is extraordinary – you are extraordinary," someone said to him. "You really think so? It's only my vision of the country," was Lemieux's simple reply, confirming the aptness of the exhibition's title.

### Commission and inspiration

In a commemorative stamp the image must serve the needs of the subject. Although the subject had been imposed, it was a natural and comfortable choice for Lemieux, whose work as a whole constitutes a personal interpretation of the country.

For several years Lemieux painted from memory, his store of images having been sufficiently large to allow him to search his inner self for vision, feeling, and inspiration. Nevertheless, three of these paintings created in the studio are based on photographs: *New Brunswick, Newfoundland,* and *Northwest Territories*. For certain parts of the country he was less familiar with, Lemieux steeped himself in local scenes before attempting his own interpretation.

### Interpreting a work of art

A work of art can be viewed from many different angles. It is a form of communication to which two individuals bring their separate interpretations. Artists expresses themselves through their work: they send out a message. Observers experience certain feelings facing the work: they receive the

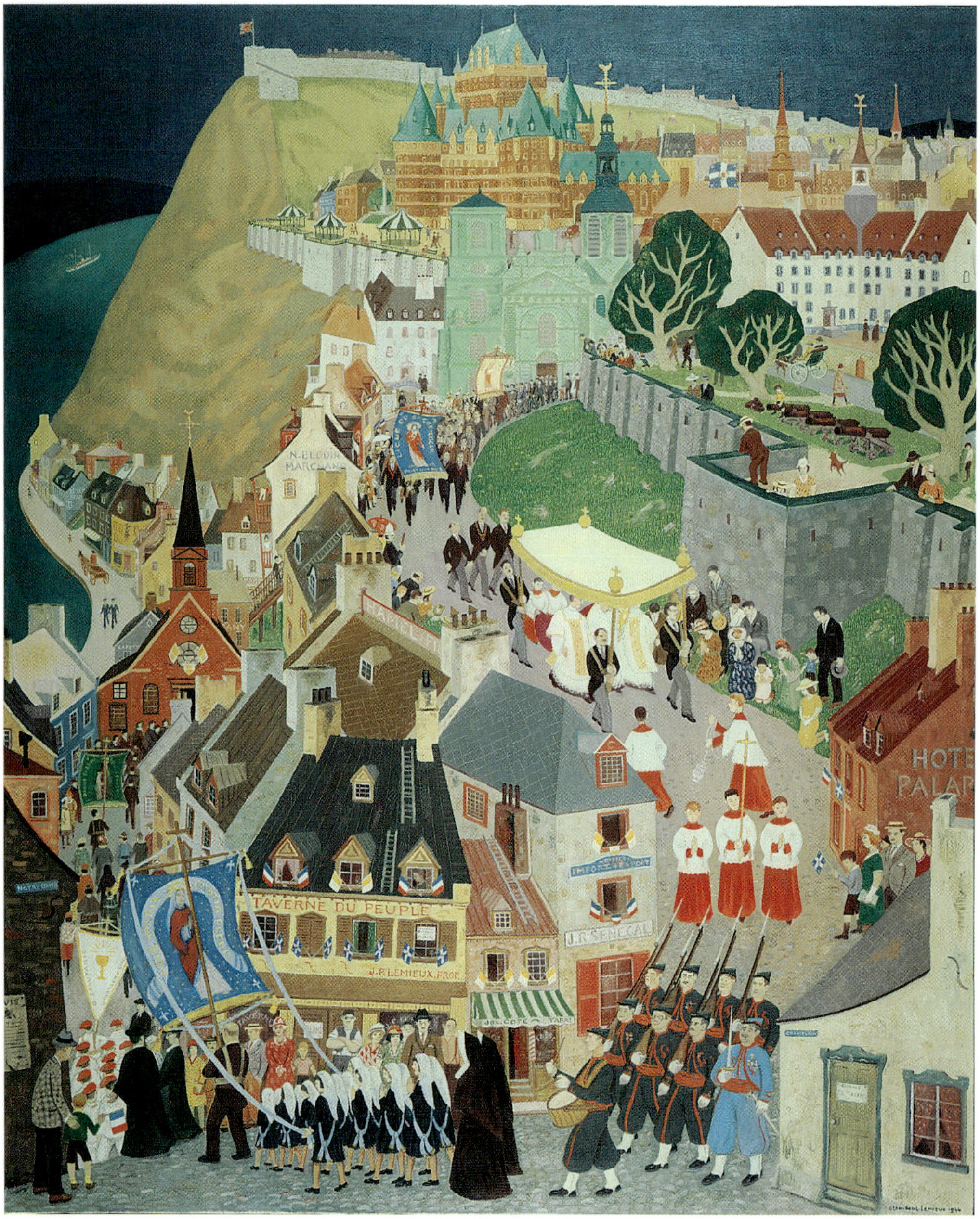


*Fête-Dieu in Quebec City*
1944
Musée du Québec

*I could never paint abroad.*
*I need to be here.*

Lemieux, 1961

message. The whole operation is very subjective, being based on the sensibilities and personal visions of artist and observer. Given any artist, interpreting a theme is almost infinitely variable, and different individuals can perceive one and the same work of art in a multitude of ways.

Although looking at and understanding a work of art is an individual endeavour based on emotion, one can attempt to analyze the effort involved by separating out some of the levels of interpretation – functional, expressive, and aesthetic. Any work of art that has an apparent function, that expresses something, and that conforms to certain aesthetic criteria will likely satisfy both intellect and emotion and remain a lasting work.

## Artistic themes

In order to explain the theme of a work or series of works, it is necessary first to define its functional and expressive purpose. The theme is the set of forms in which artists clothe their vision – the means by which they expresses themselves. The theme is something that is repeated and yet remains diversified and varied.

The repertoire of images in Lemieux's work revolves around two major themes – space and time. As the artist explained, we can never remove ourselves from these two realities; we always occupy a certain space, while the effects of time are inescapable.

## Space

For the purpose of these twelve paintings, space is Canada, which Lemieux defines by bringing out the physical characteristics of particular places. Water is present in seven of the twelve paintings, mountains in two, open plains in three. The vastness of the land is captured by horizontal treatment and the use of perspective. Several naturalistic elements are depicted or their presence is felt, though one major element – the forest – is missing.

Lemieux divides his images between town and country. *Quebec, Nova Scotia, Ontario,* and *British Columbia* illustrate the city. *New Brunswick* and *Newfoundland* depict villages; *Northwest Territories,* a few buildings. *Manitoba, Saskatchewan, Alberta,* and *Yukon* are set in the countryside.

The choice of season also expresses the painter's vision of space. Winter represents the province of Quebec, Quebec City, and Saskatchewan, while summer is a symbol of British Columbia.

> *I paint space as I feel it, and if I did it any other way, I'd be lying. It just wouldn't ring true.*
>
> Lemieux, 1972

## Time

Lemieux also locates his paintings in time, capturing a fleeting instant on his canvas. For these visions of Canada, he does so by defining a moment of the day, of the year, a moment long past, or a moment he has drawn from his own memories.

*His Canada* favours the daytime, and only two of the paintings feature a nocturnal scene. *Prince Edward Island* is pervaded by the mystery of the night, and Alberta, by a dreamlike quality. For *Nova Scotia* and *Quebec,* Lemieux harks back to a time when cities had a more human dimension, which he preferred. In *Prince Edward Island,* he takes us back a hundred years by means of a historical image.

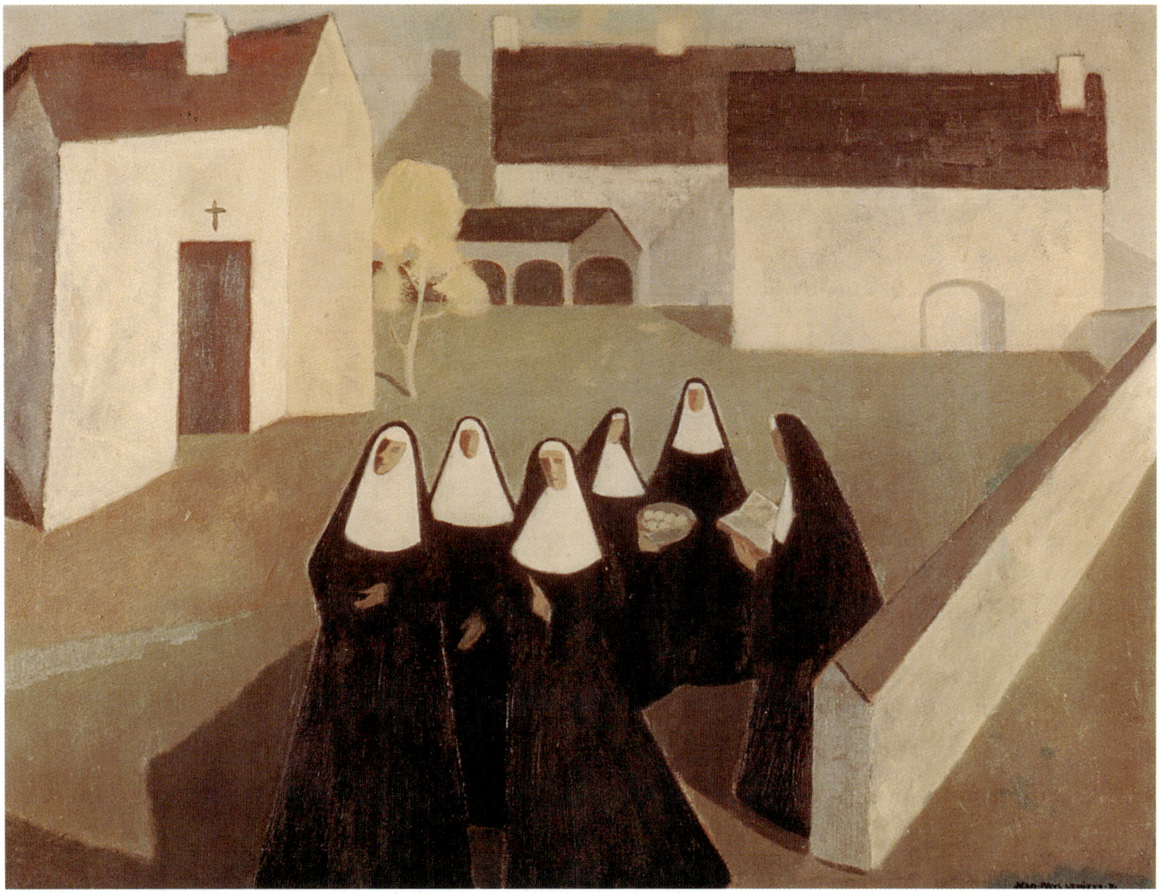

*The Ursuline Nuns,* 1951
Musée du Québec

*After 1956 and a year in France, I no longer saw things as before, I'd developed a completely different vision ... a vision that emphasized the horizontal ... I'd never noticed the extent to which our country is horizontal.*

Lemieux, 1961

The seasons, too, mark the passage of time, and Lemieux is conscious of their never-ending cycle. The critics have often labelled him a painter of the winter. This series belies that observation, for in his depiction of a country that usually brings to mind winter and northerly latitudes, he executed eight summer scenes and only four winter ones.

In *Saskatchewan,* Lemieux returns to a symbol for time: trains. The instant at which a train passes is fleeting, and we are helpless to stop either the hurtling train or the march of time itself.

> *What haunts me the most is time ... time passing by ... time already past ... the very dimension of time. Time as it slips away. And man confronted by the passage of time.*
>
> Lemieux, 1972

## Human figures

Lemieux often places a human figure in these renditions of space and time, and has created many paintings featuring figures superimposed on a background, or in a landscape. *His Canada* seems at first glance to be a collection of landscapes, but closer inspection reveals numerous figures.

Those featured in this series are almost all anonymous, with little to distinguish them – they are more like extras than major characters. A number of them have turned their backs to the onlooker, as if they themselves were looking at the landscape created by the painter. Do they nevertheless serve to create a more intimate rapport between the work and the spectator who is a witness to their story? An emotional response to these works and the feelings that emerge corresponds in part to the emotion expressed by the characters. The visions of the country Lemieux offers through these figures are positive ones. There is much joy in these paintings, as if the space and time depicted by the painter symbolized an untroubled interlude in peaceful country. Isolation, solitude, confrontation with the physical surroundings give way to a more carefree and hopeful attitude, except perhaps in *Quebec,* where the figure is depicted with a curved back. The pictures communicate a sense of the painter's nostalgia for a time long past, but little evidence of sadness.

*Saskatchewan* and *Prince Edward Island* are inhabited by the most compelling figures – real Lemieux characters. The Fathers of Confederation in *Prince Edward Island* impress us with their solemnity and a kind of historic grandeur. The figure in *Saskatchewan* is striking in his simplicity and naïvety; he is happy and seems to approach the spectator, reducing the vast plain to human dimensions.

*Yukon* depicts children; *Prince Edward Island, Alberta, Quebec,* and *Nova Scotia,* adults. For the seven other pictures, Lemieux leaves the interpretation up to the spectator. Do we find children elsewhere who, like those in *Yukon,* contribute to an image of happiness?

## Stereotyped images or simplicity of language

Several of the themes and symbols chosen by Lemieux to depict the provinces are well-worn clichés. This is true of the Fathers of Confederation for Prince Edward Island, the Quebec City skyline for the province of Quebec, the CN Tower for Ontario, and the Halifax clock tower for Nova Scotia. Sometimes the cliché lies in particular elements of the paintings: grain elevator, field of wheat, Inuk. Elsewhere, Lemieux shies away from such commonplaces: no mountains for British Columbia, no snow and cold for the Yukon, no beaches for the Atlantic provinces.

Lemieux "paints space as he feels it." Wherever clichés have served his purpose, he has used them. Not a painter who resorts to complicated or obscure symbols, his language is simple, his work open and accessible.

> *Although I don't make my horizons perfectly horizontal, this isn't because of any obsession of mine, but simply because they never are perfectly horizontal. The horizon always tilts, to the left or to the right; when you walk, the horizon sways back and forth, breathes in a way.*
>
> Lemieux, c. 1960

## Technique

Before exploring the meaning and subject of a work of art, the observer is struck first of all by the technique. The artist manipulates colour, line, and volume to produce a two-dimensional image that will create the illusion of three dimensions and serve as a vehicule for a certain theme. Each observer who confronts a work of art perceives these elements in a different order. The question as to whether a certain technique is pleasing or successful invites a highly subjective combined response from observer and artist.

As part of the artist's overall body of work, the twelve paintings *His Canada* share a common technique. Lemieux expresses himself with certain resources: a limited palette, simple shapes, restrained lines, the paint applied in short or long rectangular strokes that barely touch each other – all in a perspective that attempts to convey the sweep of the horizon and the vastness of the land.

Yet there are some innovations of technique. The paint is applied thinly, almost without texture. Blue, long absent from Lemieux's palette, appears in several of the paintings. Lemieux paints in a relaxed and easy manner, less concerned with purity of colour and line. He is undisturbed by the occasional imperfection, such as a pencil line showing through the paint. Some of these same features of colour and form are also found in the series *The Return of Maria Chapdelaine* (1981).

Although these paintings were created on a small scale for reproduction on postage stamps, they were composed in the same manner as some of the larger-scale works that are best appreciated by standing well back. Aesthetically speaking, they are more interesting from a certain distance, like Lemieux's bigger canvases.

> *I paint because I like to paint. I have no theories. In my landscapes and my characters I try to express the solitude we all have to live with, and in each painting, the inner world of my memories. My external surroundings only interest me because they allow me to paint my inner world.*
>
> Lemieux, 1967

# His Canada

## The provinces and territories

# *Quebec*

Lemieux chose Quebec City, his hometown, to illustrate the province of Quebec. He took the liberty of depicting the skyline as it was at the turn of the century, without the skyscrapers. The scene is reminiscent of *January in Quebec City* (1965), *A Fine Winter* (1966), and a number of other works that feature a view of Quebec City in the background.

The outline of the city, with its upper and lower town, is accentuated by several large masses: Cape Diamant and the Citadel on the left, the Château Frontenac in the centre, and the Seminary on the right. The ferry is crossing the ice-covered St. Lawrence. In the foreground a truncated figure walks along the wharf. A pale winter sun lights the scene.

The pictorial presentation in horizontal planes – sky, upper town, lower town, river, wharf – is a favourite of Lemieux's. The static effect of this composition is broken only by the boat and the figure, which are in motion. The scene is frozen in the bitter winter cold.

The beige and grey sky with just a hint of blue, the white of Cape Diamant, the cliff, and the river, the mixture of whites and greys that suggests ice floes drifting in the water – Lemieux's winter colours convey the impression of cold and are the right choices for depicting a Quebec City winter.

In interpreting *Quebec,* Lemieux has relied on an iconography that most Quebeckers and many Canadians associate with Quebec City. The Citadel, the fortifications, the Price Building, the buildings in the lower town from which the steeple of Notre-Dame-des-Victoires emerges are only suggested, but even an inexperienced eye will recognize *la vielle capitale*. Anyone from Quebec City or Lévis will probably identify the red patch in the background as a coastguard ship and will appreciate the details supplied by the painter's keen eye. Lemieux interprets, but remains faithful to the larger realities. The omnipresent river occupies more than half the picture, the Citadel and Château Frontenac dominate, the fortifications are also part of the scene. Lemieux has respected the popular imagery of Quebec City.

*Quebec City is easy. I've done it so often. It's a winter city, not a summer city. Quebec City in winter is much more Quebec for me. It was pretty before all the skyscrapers appeared. I don't like skyscrapers, so all I put in was the Price Building. It was the first skyscraper in Quebec City. It's Quebec City as seen from Lévis, the same vista that Morrice and Cullen once painted.*

Lemieux, 1984

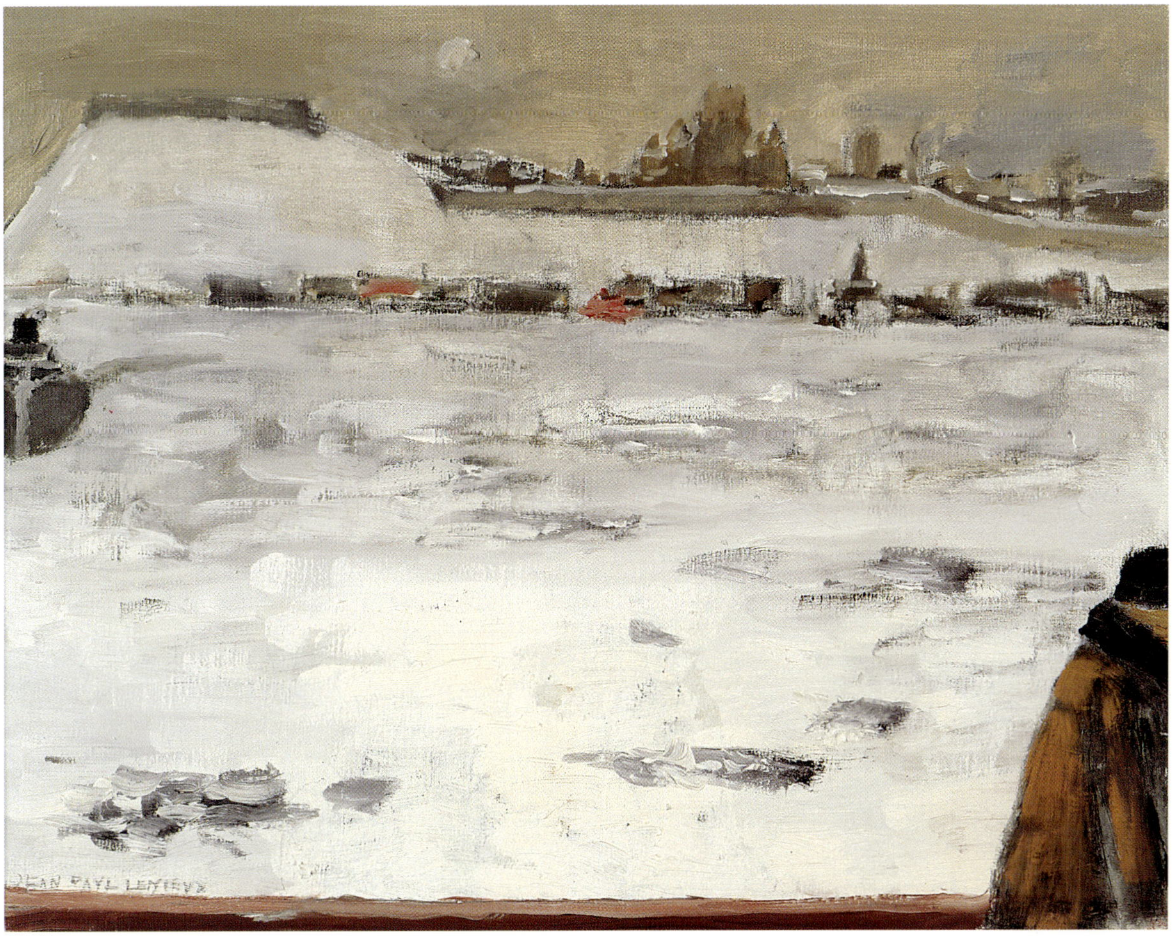


*Quebec,* 1982
Oil on canvas, 40.5 x 50.6 cm
Gift of the artist, 1983
National Archives of Canada

# *Nova Scotia*

The Citadel clock tower in Halifax is the image that arises from Lemieux's memory to represent Nova Scotia. It was a nostalgic choice because of Lemieux's interest in the Duke of Kent, who had the tower constructed. It was this same Duke who gave his name to Kent House, where Lemieux spent his childhood summers. The tower dominates the scene, occupying almost the whole height and more than half the width of the picture's surface. The composition also includes several buildings in the port, the waters of the bay, the shoreline, a few birds, and a boat. A painter is shown in one corner.

The colours – grey-blue for the sky, blue and green for the water, browns, greys, taupes for the tower, buildings, and shore – make up Lemieux's traditional palette. But the bright blue of the painter's clothing is a new colour.

The paint is applied thinly, allowing the canvas and pencil sketching to show through. The buildings of the port are imprecise, giving the impression that they had been retouched several times. Unlike several other figures in this series who are surrounded by a slightly blurred halo, the figure here seems to have been firmly placed from the very beginning.

*Nova Scotia* is one of only two vertical paintings in the series, although Lemieux controls the perspective by his use of horizontal lines.

Of the series, the painting is the most difficult to place in the body of the painter's work. Lemieux rarely features architecture in the foreground. *Pisa* (1965) was devoted to a single building, but in general, the artist uses architecture to create an atmosphere or to set a scene, as in *Tribute to Nelligan, The New Year's Day Visit* (1971), or *June Wedding* (1972).

*Nova Scotia* recalls some of Lemieux's early style. The tower is depicted with such an abundance of detail – bells, shutters, windows, columns, clock face and hands – and is so faithfully rendered that one might conclude the artist had used a photograph to revive his memories.

Is the figure in the foreground a self-portrait of the artist painting the work? An anonymous character, without visible emotion, the figure confirms Lemieux's interesting vantage point.

The theme is interpreted in a contradictory manner. The artist's personal vision is barely present in his rendering of the tower, whereas he takes considerable licence in the way he depicts Halifax itself. He has chosen an angle that excludes the skyscrapers, allowing us to see the port and an undeveloped part of the Dartmouth shore beyond the Citadel. Nevertheless, the tower remains in the heart of downtown.

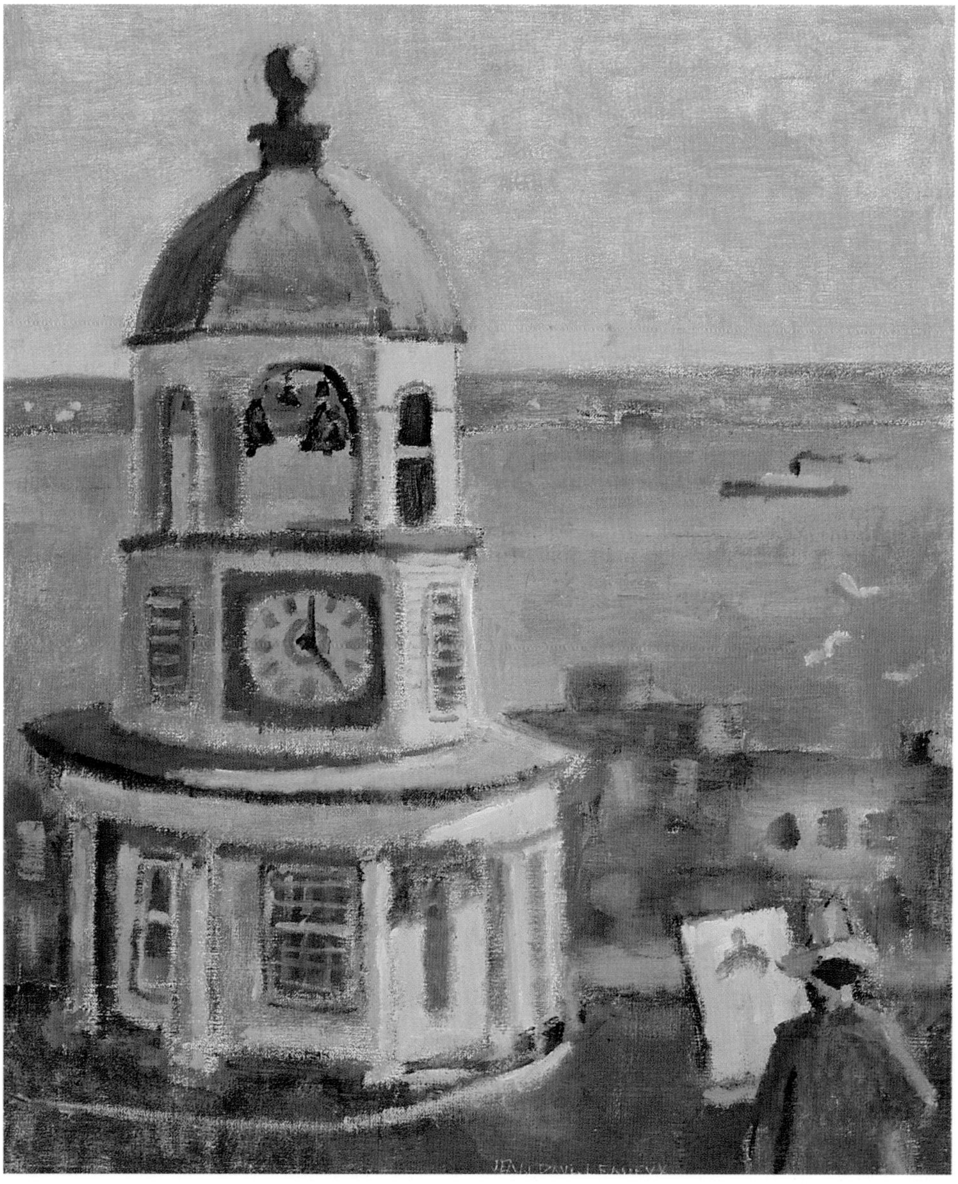

*Nova Scotia,* 1982
Oil on canvas, 50.7 x 40.7 cm
Gift of the artist, 1983
National Archives of Canada

# *Yukon*

This picture can be summed up in a few words: several children dance in a circle, accompanied by an adult, with mountains in the background.

The locale is not precisely determined as it is in several of the other pictures in the series, but the physical surroundings are nevertheless conveyed by the use of colour and compositional elements. In the background, two mountain ranges, one in blue and white, the other in grey and white, stand out against a grey sky. In the foreground, the large bare surface suggests the tundra in its hues of ochre and olive. The two horizontal planes are separated by an imprecisely drawn line.

A group of children, symmetrically organized, occupies the centre of the picture, neither arrangement typical for Lemieux. The foreground is coloured in the same browns, ochre, and olive as the background, with additional shades of red, orange, blue, and a touch of pink. These lively hues make Yukon the most colourful picture in the series.

The pencil sketching is quite evident behind the group of children and becomes a distraction when the observer stands close to the picture. The paint is applied in very thin layers and the larger surfaces seem to have been brushed over hurriedly.

Nevertheless, the work is resonant, appealing, and charged with movement and emotion. Does the picture as a whole convey the feeling that the painter was trying to communicate: a sense of hope, symbolized by these children?

*This is a joyful painting. We always think of something sad when we think of Yukon, because of the gold rush. I wanted to leave the onlooker with an image of hope ... our children.*

Lemieux, 1984

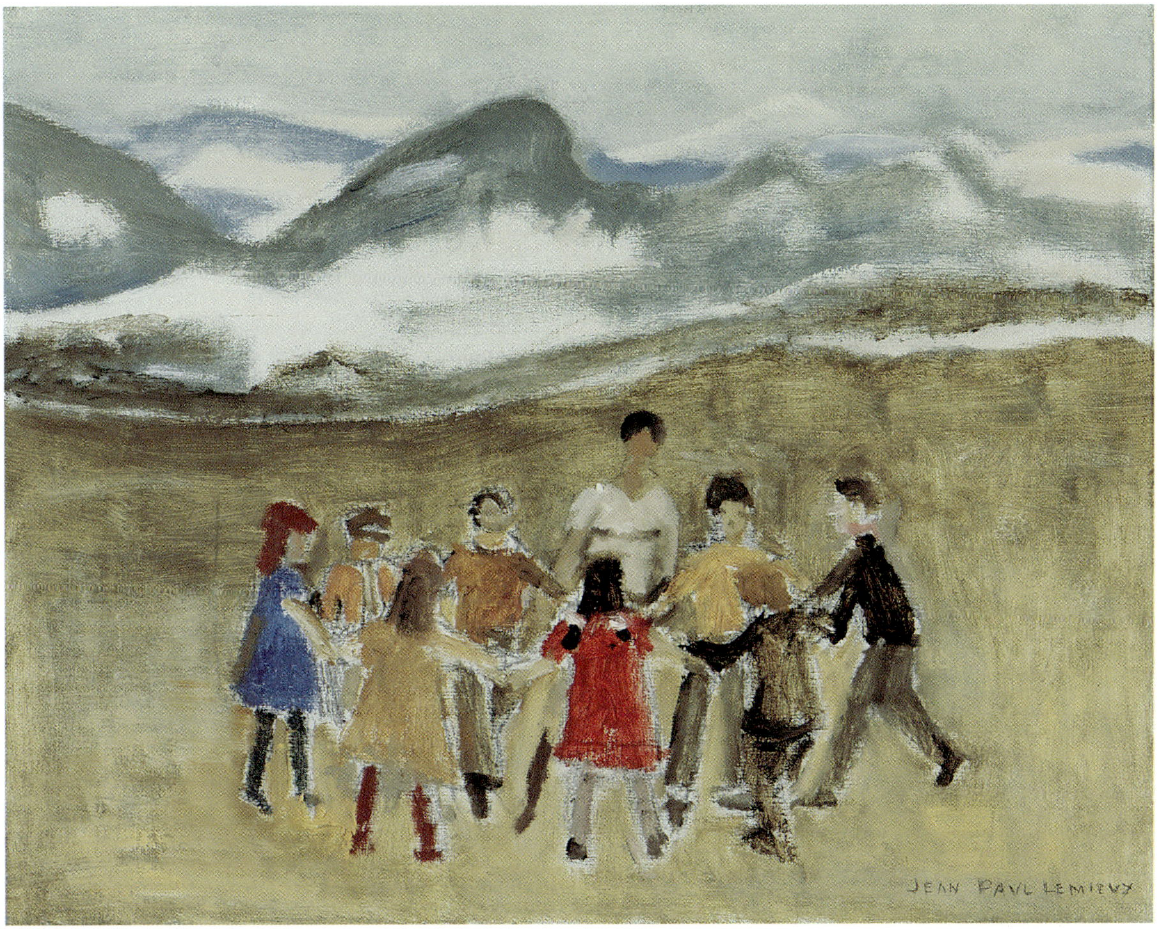


*Yukon,* 1982
Oil on canvas, 40.5 x 50.3 cm
Gift of the artist, 1983
National Archives of Canada

# *Ontario*

The CN Tower, symbol of Toronto, allows us to identify a scene that might otherwise be representative of any one of several North American cities. Lemieux utilizes the standard cliché: the view of the tourist who sails on the lake or strolls along the beaches of the Toronto Islands. The water reminds us that the city is situated on the shores of Lake Ontario. The picture is composed of few elements: the tower, the city skyline, the lake, some greenery, and two human figures.

Lemieux offers a realistic view of Toronto. The city is compact, and from the lake the horizon is not visible. The painter places a horizontal line in the centre of the composition; it tilts slightly and causes the city to tilt as well. It is one of Lemieux's most cherished principles that his horizons not be perfectly horizontal. Although the picture is vertical, the perspective is a horizontal one: beach, lake, buildings, sky are layered in horizontal rings. Apart from the tower, the various shapes are not identified. Nor, for that matter, are the foreground figures, though they add a warm, human dimension to the cold, impersonal big city.

The colours are cool: blue and green dominate sky and skyline. Lemieux adds brown for the water of the lake, which does not have the limpid quality of the water in *New Brunswick, Nova Scotia,* and *British Columbia*. The colours of the bathing suits lend some variety to the cooler hues with touches of ochre, red, and white. A summery climate is suggested by the soft, diffuse quality of the light.

The paint is applied in very thin layers, which allows the canvas to show through. Shapes are circumscribed not by outlines, but by areas of colour that do not come into contact. As with *Quebec,* a number of the elements border on abstraction, but taken together they form a figurative composition. Therein lies the magic of the Lemieux touch. Everything appears so simple, so easy, yet few artists achieve the same results using such pared-down resources.

Lemieux had already employed this method of drawing the city and its lookalike buildings in *The City* (1956), *Metropolis* (1960), *Snowbound City* (1963), and in a number of watercolours from 1972 that depict North America in the year 2082.

Here Lemieux does not go back in time, as he does for Halifax and Quebec City. His contemporary interpretation of Toronto conforms to the popular image of Ontario typified by this city with the greatest concentration of people in Canada, even though the farmlands of the south and the forests of the north are a dramatically different reality.

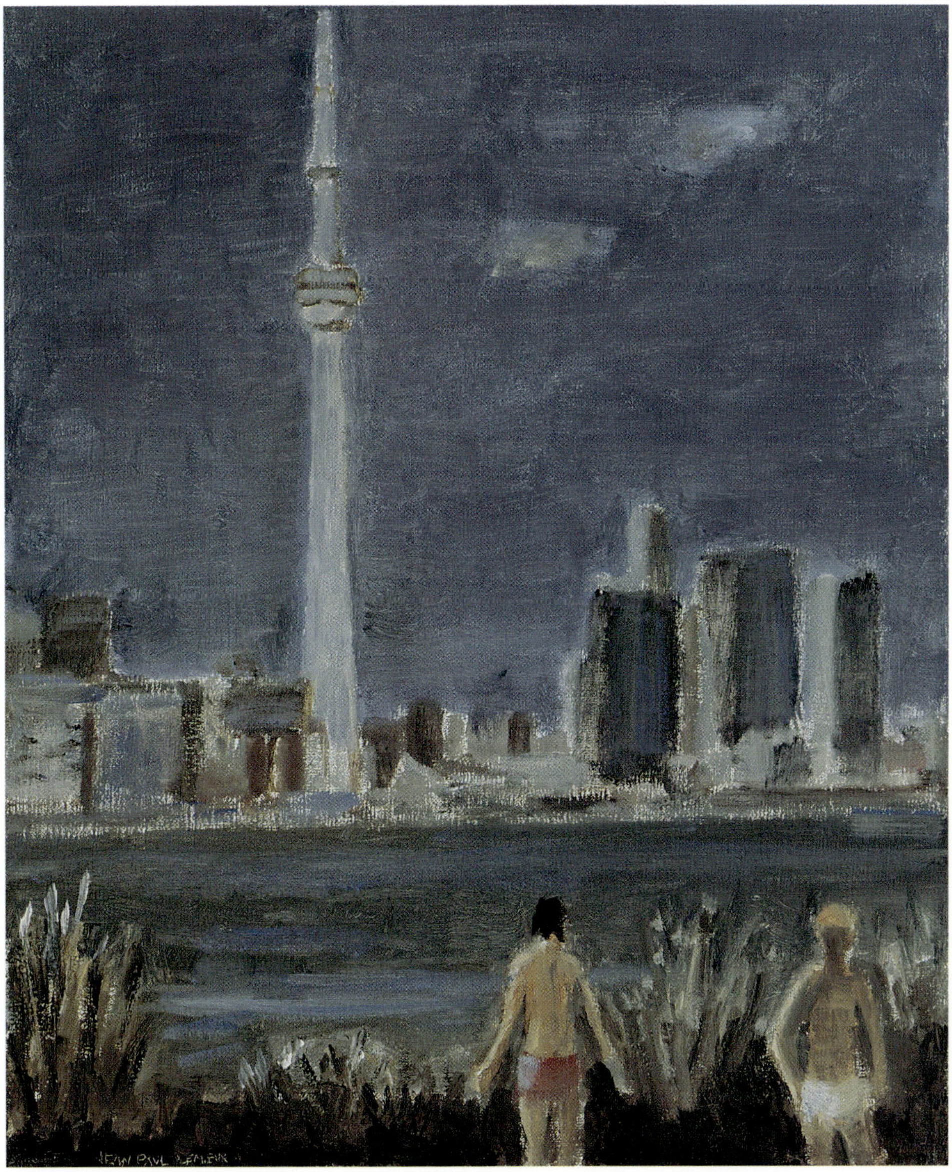

*Ontario,* 1982
Oil on canvas, 50.6 x 40.5 cm
Gift of the artist, 1983
National Archives of Canada

# *British Columbia*

English Bay, a sunny beach in the heart of Vancouver, is the vision that Lemieux depicts on this canvas titled *British Columbia.* The bay forms a semicircle with the beach taking the same shape. The skyscrapers of West Vancouver and the headland of Point Grey close off the scene, a classic vista featured in all the Vancouver tourist guides. The painter managed to retain accurate memories from a trip taken during the 1950s. Any temptation we may feel to compare this painting with his other compositions disappears when we are confronted by the links to this actual place.

Lemieux organizes the masses in horizontal planes: beach, bay, headlands, buildings, and sky. Because of the long curve of the beach, however, the perspective changes. There is a great deal of depth, and the eye moves easily from one plane to another in the picture. The sailboat, the waves rendered by a simple white brush stroke, the strolling figure, the distant figures – mere dabs of colour – at the end of the beach, lend still more movement. Nevertheless, a feeling of calm and peace in the heart of a large city pervades this composition.

The painter's eye has caught and rendered the vibrant and intense light peculiar to the Pacific Coast, so different from the cold luminescence that envelops the Eastern provinces and Prairies in the winter, which Lemieux captures so well. The spectator feels bathed in a radiance that owes more to Gauguin than to Lemieux.

But the dominant colours still belong to Lemieux's palette: a Lemieux grey-blue for the sky and a little darker shade for the water; yellow ochre Lemieux for the beach; brown and olive. The orange in the foreground is striking and allows the hot colours to dominate and diffuse a golden glow that creates a sunny environment.

As far as technique is concerned, *British Columbia* is very much a part of this series: the same application of paint, the same indistinct lines around the human figure in the foreground, canvas and sketching visible to the eye. Outlines are entirely absent, and the forms take their shape from the organization of very simple masses of colour. The brushwork has an unstudied look.

For Lemieux, this portrayal of Vancouver evokes happy memories of a summer he once spent there. It is an image that will strike a sympathetic chord with many inhabitants of Vancouver and British Columbia, for English Bay is a spot they love and are proud to call their own.

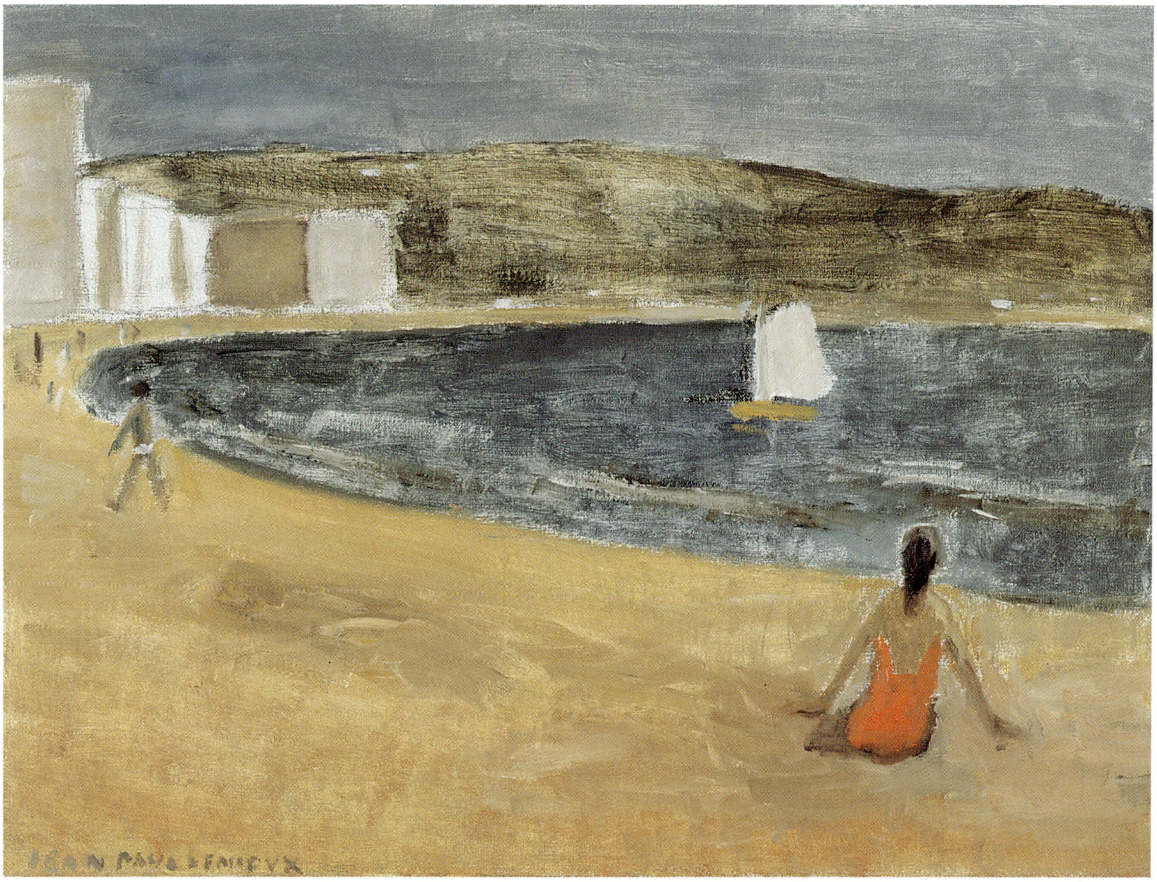

*British Columbia,* 1982
Oil on canvas, 38.8 x 50.7 cm
Gift of the artist, 1983
National Archives of Canada

# *Prince Edward Island*

All the works in *His Canada* contain references to geography, with the exception of *Prince Edward Island.* Here Lemieux suggests a voyage back in time to 1864, and depicts the Fathers of Confederation at the Charlottetown conference. This is a small-scale version of a mural executed in 1964 for the Confederation Centre of the Arts in Charlottetown.

In 1964 the critics pronounced *Charlottetown Revisited* one of Lemieux's masterpieces, and this new version from 1982, despite differences in composition and scale, is equally successful – a classic Lemieux.

Three figures in capes, tall black hats, and white collars monopolize the entire right side and foreground of the picture. The horizon, in the lower quarter of the picture, abuts against the figures. A building with a triangular façade suggests Province House, while the trees and moon complete the composition. The colours – black, yellow, and olive – are ones that the painter had mastered, yellow in particular a colour that he made his own.

In comparison with *Charlottetown Revisited,* Lemieux made several changes: the figures are rearranged, the building is off centre and less classical in its lines, two trees are added, and the light appears nocturnal. The composition has the same technical characteristics as the other pictures in the series: colour applied in thin layers, visible canvas and sketching, a slight blurring around the heads of the figures, few contour lines.

The real enchantment comes from the spatial organization and the light. The three people in the foreground are in fact arranged on three different levels, from the centre to the right-hand side. The first figure is turned at a three-quarter angle, the face in profile; the second is facing us, as is the third, but with the face in three-quarter profile. The interlocking planes, the horizon broken in the middle of the picture, the small scale of the building and the trees, the dramatic lighting emanating from the rear, all direct our attention toward the figures and emphasize their solemnity. Lemieux is reconstructing an important moment from Canada's history and in doing so creates an air of gravity that arouses the spectator's emotions. The nocturnal lighting adds an even more solemn touch. In *Charlottetown Revisited* the pomp and circumstance were further marked by the classical style of the building and the lack of any reference to nature. The scene seems suspended in space and time.

By using historical symbolism for his interpretation, Lemieux has given to this often overlooked smallest province an important place in Canadian history, presenting it as the site where the idea of Confederation had its beginnings.

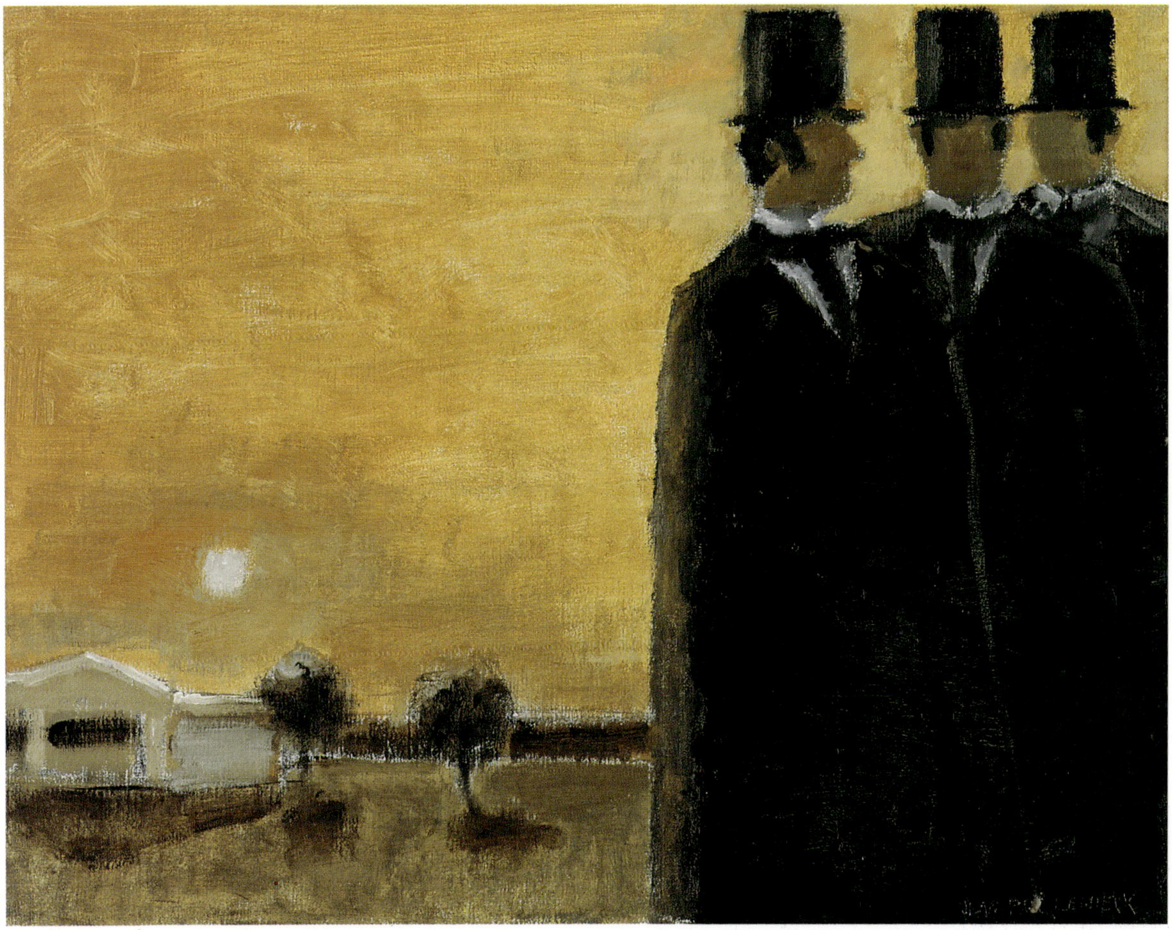

*Prince Edward Island,* 1982
Oil on canvas, 38.8 x 50.7 cm
Gift of the artist, 1983
National Archives of Canada

## *Newfoundland*

Newfoundland is represented by Îles-aux-Morts, a little village on the south coast. Never having visited the province, Lemieux depicts the village as it became known to him through a photograph by John de Visser.

The work comprises some ten buildings scattered over hilly terrain – a scene typical of Newfoundland's small outports. In the centre, where hills provide a natural protection, skaters glide over the frozen inlet. Other figures move toward the skating area. The fence, in the form of a semicircle, directs their movement. The perspective opens out to the sea, dotted with drift ice.

The palette here resembles that used in *Quebec,* where Lemieux also wanted to convey the idea of cold: beige sky, olive-coloured sea, snowy surfaces in white, beige, and grey, buildings in ochre, blue, and vermilion. The figures are executed in darker hues, except for one in red. The olive colour of the water looks surprising at first glance, but in winter the sea often takes on a dark aspect in contrast with the snow. Lemieux chose lively colours for the buildings and, whether wittingly or not, happened upon the identical shades used to paint houses in the Atlantic provinces.

The picture is organized from the centre out, a spatial organization that is quite rare in Lemieux's work, but more understandable when one realizes that the artist was inspired by a photograph. The spectator's eye alights first on the centre, then roams across the larger spaces and towards the horizon. There are many curved and sinuous lines: the shore of the bay, the fence, the line of the hills, the seashore.

Although based on a photograph as well as on the reality of the landscape, the composition nevertheless bears Lemieux's mark: his winter colours applied in thin layers, elements built up from masses of colour rather than by precise outlines. There are, however, more lines that circumscribe planes or objects than in the other pictures of the series. The horizon between sea and sky, here unusually straight, is another Lemieux trademark. The painter always opens up his perspective in a way that suggests the vastness of the land. The anonymous figures, suggested by simple strokes of the brush, still convey a sense of movement.

Lemieux confessed to having envisioned Newfoundland as a sad place with a harsh climate. Yet this is a joyful work, perhaps created to confound our preconceptions.

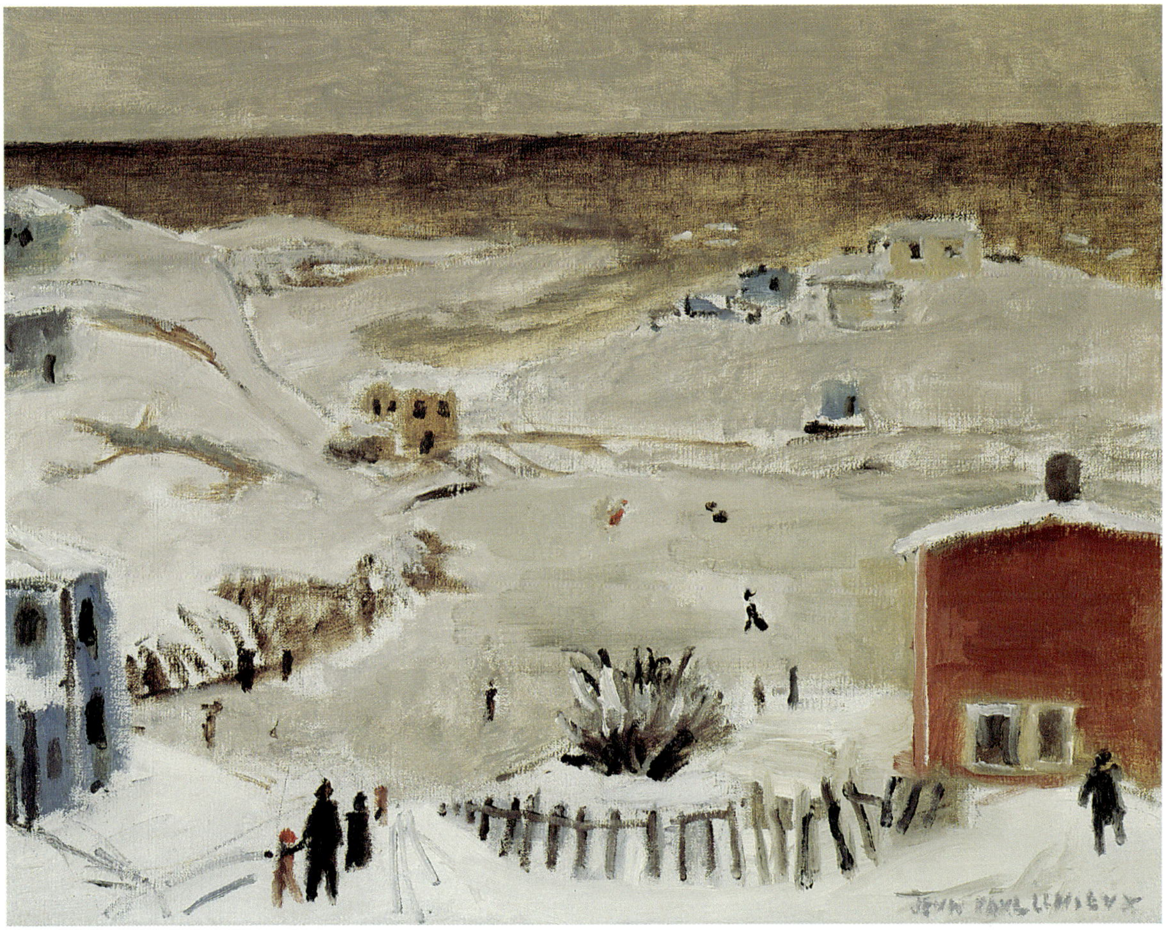


*Newfoundland,* 1982
Oil on canvas, 40.5 x 50.5 cm
Gift of the artist, 1983
National Archives of Canada

*Little isolated villages, something which will disappear no doubt. I thought: why not set the scene in winter? There's lots of snow there also, and it gets cold. It's a sad place in a sense. Even Jacques Cartier thought it was bleak.*

Lemieux, 1984

## New Brunswick

Lemieux sets the action along the Saint John River, near the town of the same name. In the foreground, he has placed three figures and a dog on the beach; in the background, a few houses, a church, clumps of trees. Between the two the river is ever-present and fills two-thirds of the composition. Horizontal lines predominate, with the beach, the river, the shore, and the sky following one another in parallel planes. Only the church steeple and the two standing figures lend a counterweight to the horizontal perspective.

The artist uses thin applications of paint, the canvas showing through in several places. A house in the centre of the picture owes its very existence to the almost total lack of paint; only two dark strokes mark its openings.

The colours are not pure. Blue is mixed with beige, yellowish ochre with olive green. The blue of the sky and the river, though touched with a little grey, contrasts with the usual greys and beiges Lemieux uses for skies and the olive he chose for the sea in *Newfoundland.* The lively colours of the bathing suits, the white of the church, the white of the canvas, and the yellow sand combine to produce a pastel image in the spirit of summer.

The houses, which one can barely make out along the river bank, echo several of Lemieux's canvases such as *The Orphan* (1956) and *Small Town* (1963) in which the town or village is relegated to the background,

In painting *New Brunswick,* Lemieux was inspired by a photograph. It is difficult to say whether he chose this photograph because it corresponded to his own ideas on perspective, or whether he transformed the view to suit his own purpose. His interpretation of the province is centred entirely on physical reality. Lemieux singles out the Saint John River as an important natural element worthy of symbolizing New Brunswick.

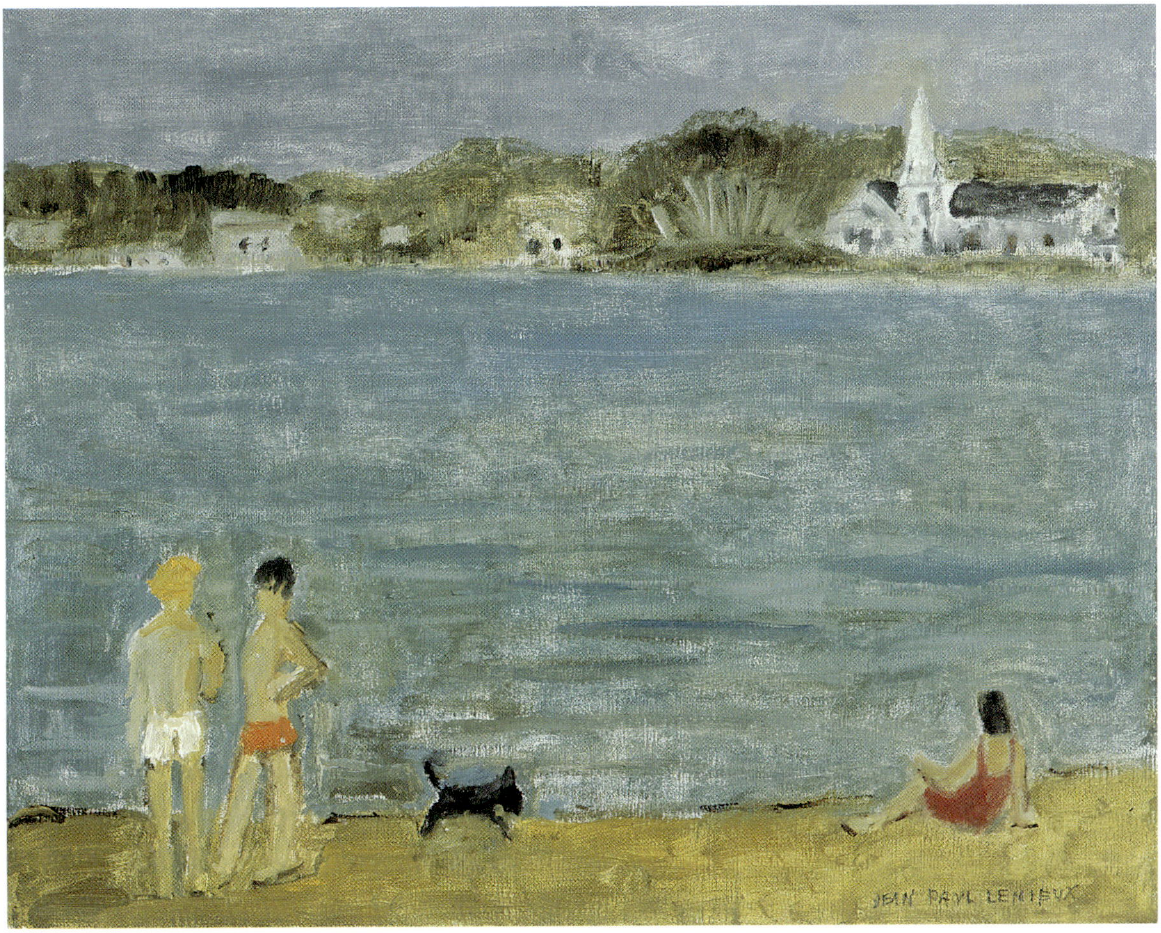


*New Brunswick,* 1982
Oil on canvas, 40.4 x 50.5 cm
Gift of the artist, 1983
National Archives of Canada

# Saskatchewan

One could describe *Saskatchewan* as a typical Lemieux – a figure in a landscape. The eye alights on three main elements: a truncated figure, a train, and a grain elevator. But there is also the space defined by the landscape and the passage of time symbolized by the train, soon to disappear, taking with it a fleeting moment of time. *Saskatchewan* belongs among Lemieux's most successful works.

The composition is typical of the artist. In the foreground, the figure occupies approximately one quarter of the available space. Behind him stretches a vast plain. The perspective leads us to the train as it appears on the horizon, running on an oblique track that balances this linear aspect. The horizon "breathes," as Lemieux would say, in that it is not perfectly horizontal, but a little curved in the middle. The grain elevator provides a counterweight to the figure.

The figure is part of the best Lemieux tradition. He gazes out at us with feeling, overcoming any sense of anonymity. His face is built up from masses of colour with little linear quality, yet his body is precisely outlined. He is reminiscent of Maria Chapdelaine or François Paradis, previous creations of Lemieux's brush. He also bears a family resemblance to the Julie of *Julie and the Universe,* to the figures of *Orion* (1967) and *Winter Solstice* (1961), and to all the other figures in his paintings who are there to tell a story and whose role it is to express the relationship between human beings and the space engulfing them. How closely is the landscape related to this figure? The figure in *Saskatchewan* is happy, carefree, and seemingly unburdened by the bitter cold winter.

*The Noon Train, The White Fields* (1956), *The Road That Leads Nowhere,* as well as paintings such as *The Silence* (1976), *Crossing the Peribonka River* (1981), and *The Church of Peribonka* (1981) all use the same perspective and succeed in conveying the vastness of the land. Like *Saskatchewan,* these works point to a paradox about Lemieux. How does he manage to convey such a strong sense of space and time with such an economy of means and such spare compositional elements?

Soft tones dominate: pinkish beige, yellowish beige, dusty pink, white, and beige. The entire landscape shares this unobtrusive, monochromatic quality. Even the deep red of the train derives from the same range of colours. The figure dressed in blue stands out against these muted shades, yet is linked to the landscape by the colour of his swarthy complexion and frost-nipped cheeks as well as his contours.

There are no false starts evident in the technique. The paint is applied fairly thickly and covers the sketching completely. The vast white surface is textured, as snowscapes usually are in Lemieux's work. Nothing has been covered or redone. The picture seems completely natural.

The artist's interpretation fits the popular preconceptions about the province: long bleak winters as much as endless fields of grain. The train strikes a historical note because of its role in Saskatchewan's development

To the question "what is a Lemieux?" we could simply reply "a painting like *Saskatchewan.*"

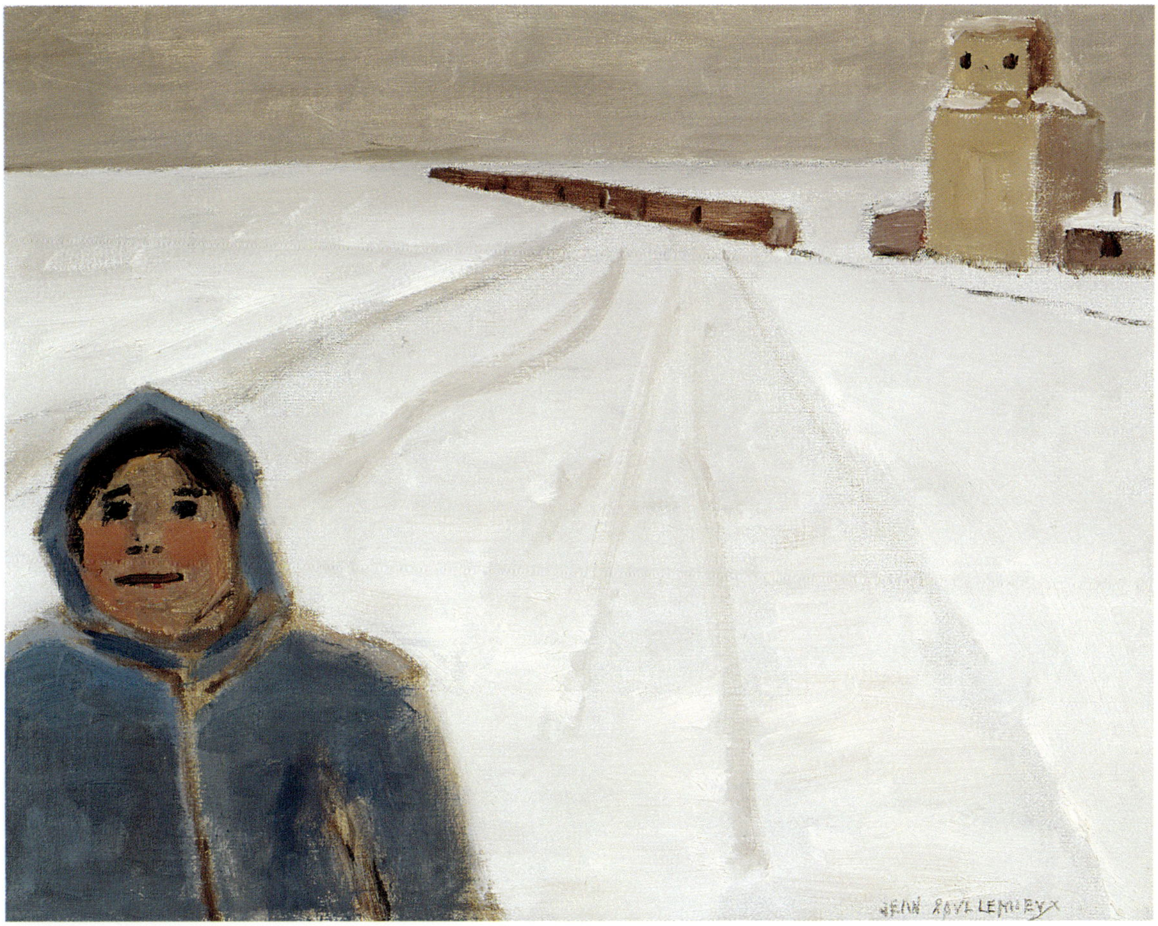

*Saskatchewan,* 1982
Oil on canvas, 40.4 x 50.5 cm
Gift of the artist, 1983
National Archives of Canada

*This is Saskatchewan with its grain elevators. I was tired of painting fields of wheat. Instead I decided to depict winter, which is so cold there. The presence of the snow changes the whole painting.*

Lemieux, 1984

# *Manitoba*

Lemieux has chosen a rustic scene to convey his memories of Manitoba: a human figure and a few birds in a field of grain. One part of the field has been harvested, the other not – a novel depiction of this subject. The horizon line in the upper quarter of the picture opens up the perspective and creates a feeling of space, giving the picture some depth. Rather than the vast traditional fields, this painting evokes the smaller fields that may be more typical of Manitoba – fields that run up against other physical objects. Here Lemieux does not achieve the same depth found in *The White Fields* and *Landscape with Two Figures* (1965).

The facial features of the character in the foreground are not very detailed, yet the eyes are piercing and reminiscent of *Marie Gemma* (1958) and one of the women in *Three Women* (1972). While he is not anonymous like the majority of the characters in this series, neither does he rivet our attention in the same manner as the figure in Saskatchewan.

The colours are jumbled: yellow, olive brown, and ochre for the field. The blue of the sky is mixed with yellow and becomes almost green to the right of the picture. The pale, vertical strokes in the field barely resemble tall, slender stalks of grain. Once again, the paint is applied in thin layers and reveals a number of false starts. A house appears in the upper right-hand corner. The awkward alterations are evident around the figure and produce an unattractive colour.

The painter found this grain field the best means of representing Manitoba. Did his memory suggest the subject because fields are still the most common symbol of this varied province?

*What's in* Manitoba *is imaginary,*
*based on my memories of Manitoba.*
*There were so many fields.*

Lemieux, 1984

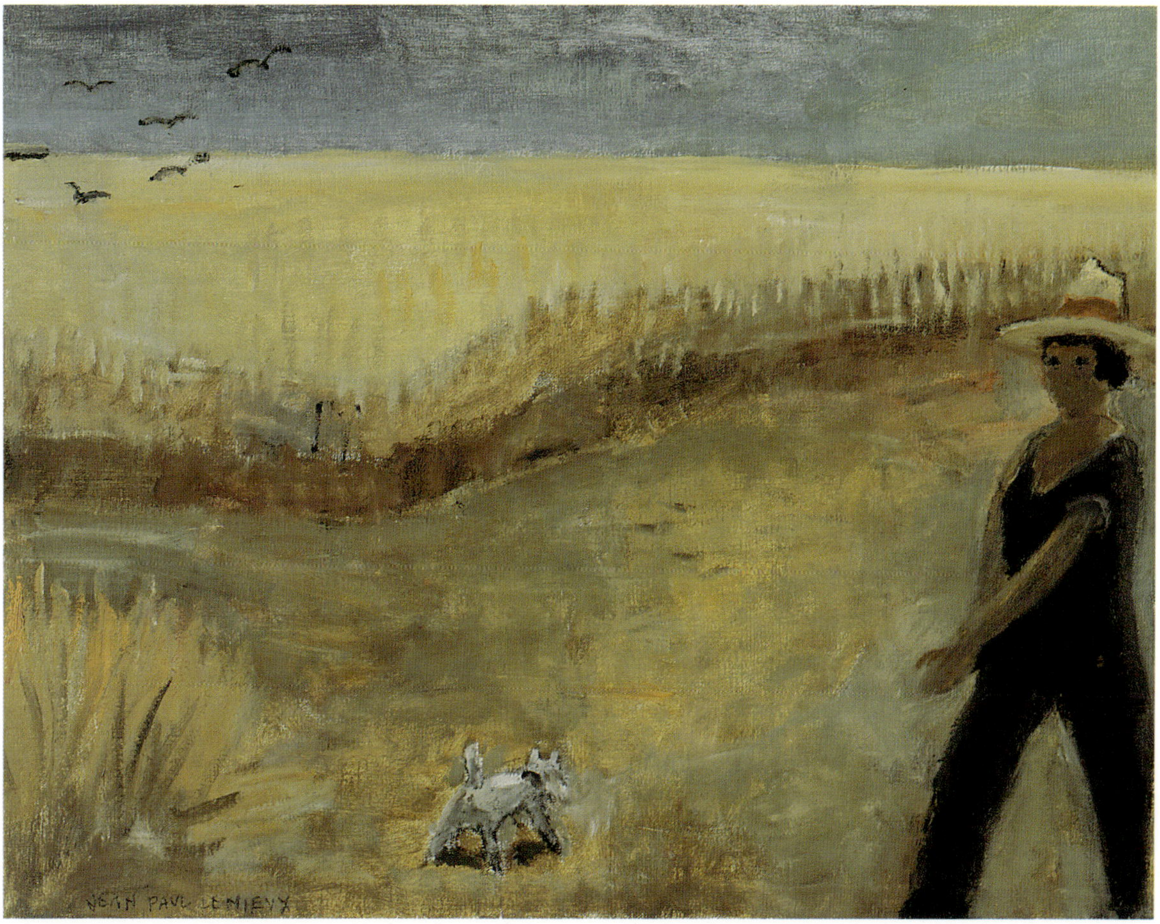


*Manitoba,* 1982
Oil on canvas, 40.4 x 50.5 cm
Gift of the artist, 1983
National Archives of Canada

## *Northwest Territories*

Lemieux found his inspiration for this scene in a photograph, yet he modified the original shot in a number of ways. The place depicted is a DEW Line radar station at Cape Parry, on Amundsen Gulf near the Arctic Circle.

The figure of an Inuk occupies the foreground. Farther back, the artist has placed a church, which he saw and liked in the original photograph, as well as two other rudimentary structures. An oblique line starts behind one of the buildings and divides the picture into two parts. In the background are the sea, dotted with drift ice, and mountains standing out against the sky along the horizon. This organization of the space into two planes – one containing a figure in a determinate time and place, and the other, a panoramic view of a vast, open space – is typical of Lemieux.

The buildings are made up of simple shapes, and the use of colours shows the same simplicity of means. Here Lemieux chooses a palette of cool colours: grey, blue mixed with grey and green, white. Only the yellow of the house on the left, a red patch near the shoreline, and the brown and ochre of the figure are distinguished from the dominant cool tones. One of the houses and the church, probably originally painted in red or blue, have been covered with a layer of white to give an impression of cold. Some forms have been eliminated by the artist, but they are still visible through the paint.

The presence of the figure lends a realistic quality to the picture. Situated at the edge of the composition as is typical in Lemieux's work, the figure's relationship with the surrounding space is not confrontational; instead it seems to be an integral part of this seemingly hostile environment.

The image Lemieux conveys here conforms to our ideas about this part of the country: small built-up areas scattered across a cold and empty landscape.

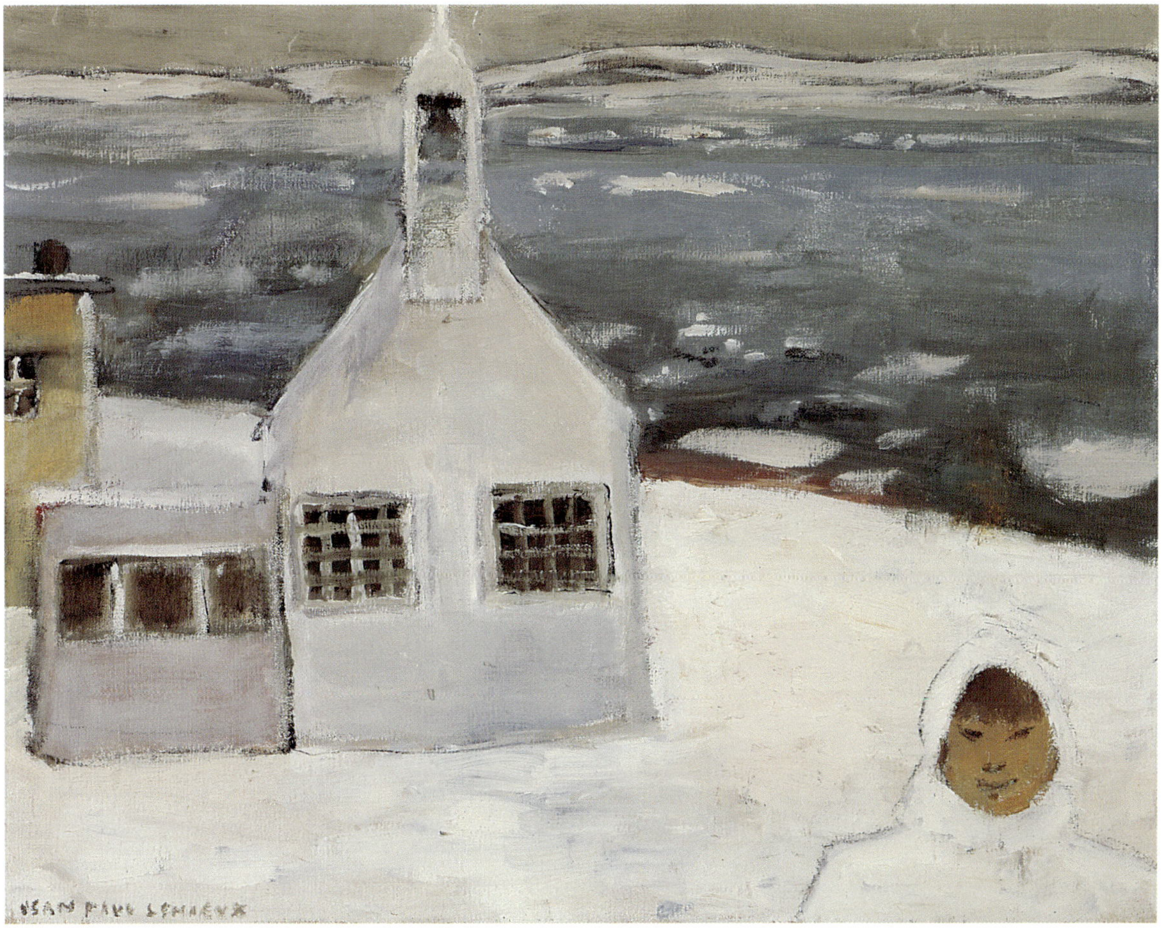


*Northwest Territories,* 1982
Oil on canvas, 40.6 x 50.5 cm
Gift of the artist, 1983
National Archives of Canada

# *Alberta*

Several years before painting this work, Lemieux executed a mural titled *The Dream*. This mural evoked the Prairies, a subject Lemieux took up again for *Alberta*. The picture shows a Prairie landscape with a reclining woman in the foreground, her back to us. Several animals are grazing on the plain. On the horizon, the foothills of the Rockies stand out against a night sky. The scene is flooded by moonlight.

Lemieux again exploits the themes of space and time. The vastness of the Prairies is conveyed by the horizon in the upper quarter of the picture, leaving three-quarters of the picture for the plain. To bring out the linear quality of this space, Lemieux arranges it in a manner that he is particularly fond of: the plain, the mountains, and the sky all form horizontal lines. A sense of time is established by the dark sky and the nocturnal light that pervades the scene with pastel shades of pink, yellow, and blue.

The picture has a certain abstract quality. The shapes are only roughly sketched: the figure is one block, the mountains are a jumble of criss-crossing colours, the animals are greatly simplified. Nevertheless, Lemieux does not quite cross the line into abstract art. The composition remains figurative in its use of perspective and its naturalistic references.

As with other paintings in this series, one senses a certain hesitation in the outline of shapes and the application of paint. Once more, Lemieux is not striving for technical perfection but rather seeks to create an atmosphere and provoke an emotional response from the observer.

Despite the nocturnal light and the presence of a number of black shapes, *Alberta,* like *Yukon,* is a colourful picture. The use of lively shades such as red and orange as well as pastel hues produces an unusual effect in this night scene. The colours are vibrant, even though the pastels of the moonlight create a soft, dreamy atmosphere.

Why this association of the dream and the Prairie province? The answer is probably a historical one. Over the course of the early twentieth century, the Western provinces represented the promise of a better world for many Canadians. For some, at least, the dream came to an abrupt end with the stock market crash of 1929.

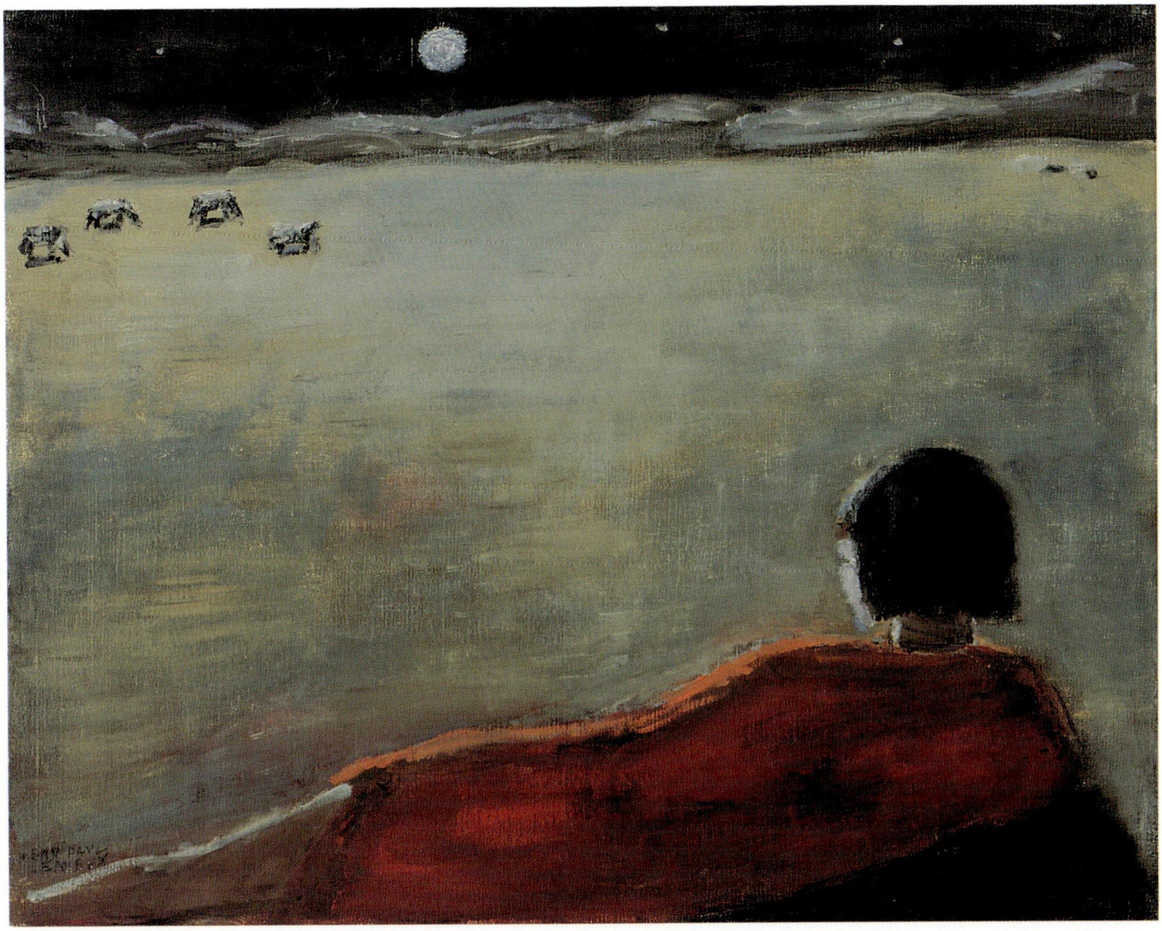

*Alberta,* 1982
Oil on canvas, 40.5 x 50.6 cm
Gift of the artist, 1983
National Archives of Canada

# *From work of art to postage stamp*

After a work of art has been selected to illustrate a stamp, the process of reproduction begins, with each stage approved by Canada Post Corporation. The images for "Canada Day 1984" were conceived by Jean Paul Lemieux and the design – that is, the melding of image and typographical signs and the layout of the block as a whole – was executed by Jean Morin and Tom Yakobina.

## Five-colour lithography

The nature of the image to be reproduced determines the production technique for a particular stamp. In Canada during the 1980s, the choice was usually for litho-offset in the case of a polychromatic work. The design is first miniaturized by photographic means and then subjected to the colour-separation process. The image is broken down into four colours: yellow, cyan (blue), magenta (red), and black. This stage is important, as a faithful reproduction of the original work depends on the quality of the colour separations. Whenever several different images are combined in a single block, the printer-lithographer must make some compromises, since the colours can never be perfectly balanced.

Each image, one for each colour, is then transferred to metal plates, which are mounted on the press. The surface of each plate is treated with an oily substance and then moistened with water. Since oil and water do not mix, the ink will adhere only to those parts of the plate that form the image. The image is transferred from the plate to a rubber cylinder and then onto paper. It is the combination or superimposition of the images produced by the four plates that gives the polychromatic image. For the "Canada Day 1984" series of stamps, a fifth colour, grey, was added to the four standard colours for the stamp's typography and inscriptions in the margins.

The printer must produce several sets of proofs before the final run: proofs for colour and for layout, on both ordinary paper and gummed paper as well as watermarked paper specially produced for postage stamps. The "Canada Day 1984" stamps were printed in sheets – perforated and cut before leaving the machine – containing twenty copies of the miniature block.

In the course of this process, a kind of artistic miracle occurs: often unknown works of art are suddenly reproduced millions of times over.

Because postage stamps have a negotiable value, just like bank notes, they are printed by companies that have designated standards of security. The printers must account for each piece of paper used, make their own inks, and destroy any part of the production run that is deemed to be of inferior quality. This can mean a trip to the incinerator for many stamps.

Despite all the proofs, approvals, and modifications, errors can still go unnoticed. In the "Canada Day 1984" series, the stamp depicting the Yukon in fact represents the Northwest Territories, and vice versa.

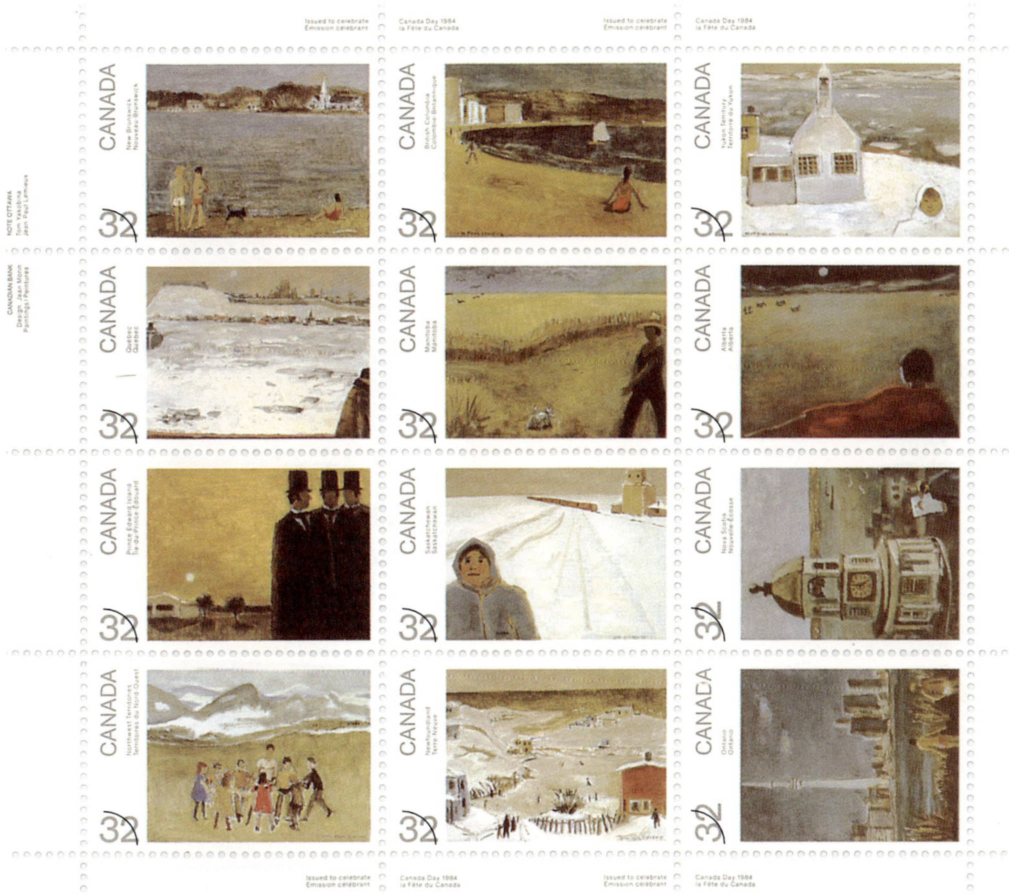

**"Canada Day 1984," miniature block of twelve stamps**

| | |
|---|---|
| Value: | 32 cents |
| Date of issue: | June 29, 1984 |
| Printer: | Canadian Bank Note Company, Ottawa |
| Print run: | 52,800,000 (4,400,000 of each design) |

Reproduced with the permission of Canada Post Corporation

# Selected exhibitions and work by Jean Paul Lemieux

**1931–42**

Participation in the Salon du printemps, Musée des beaux-arts, Montreal

**1934–54**

Participation in annual exhibitions, Royal Canadian Academy of Arts

**1937**

Student exhibitions, École des beaux-arts, Montreal

**1938**

Exhibition with Madeleine Desrosiers, Galerie Morency, Quebec City

**1946**

*Canadian Painting,* UNESCO, Paris

**1950**

Private exhibition, artist's residence, Quebec City

**1953**

Group exhibition, National Gallery of Canada, Ottawa

First solo exhibition, Palais Montcalm, Quebec City

**1956**

Solo exhibition, *La Côte d'Azur,* L'Atelier, Quebec City

**1957, 1959, 1963, 1965**

Biennales, National Gallery of Canada, Ottawa

**1957**

São Paolo Biennale, Brazil

Mural, *Medecine in Quebec City,* Laval University, Sainte-Foy

**1958**

Brussels World's Fair, Canadian Pavillion

Pittsburgh International Exhibition

Solo exhibition, Vancouver

**1959**

Solo exhibition, Galerie Denyse Delrue, Montreal

**1960**

Solo exhibition, Roberts Gallery, Toronto

Venice Biennale

Group exhibition, Stratford

**1962**

*Canadian Painters,* organized by the National Gallery of Canada, Warsaw

**1963**

Solo exhibition, Galerie Agnès Lefort, Montreal

Solo exhibition, Roberts Gallery, Toronto

*Five Canadian Painters,* Musée Galliera, Paris

*Eleven Canadian Artists,* Tate Gallery, London

**1964**

Mural, Confederation Centre of the Arts, Charlottetown

**1965**

Solo exhibition, Galerie Zannetin, Quebec City

**1966**

*Montreal Masterpieces,* presented in seven U.S. cities

Retrospective, Art Gallery of London

**1967**

*Three Hundred Years of Canadian Art,* National Gallery of Canada, Ottawa

Christmas card for UNICEF

**1967–68**

Retrospective, *Jean Paul Lemieux: 1917–1967,* Musée des beaux-arts, Montreal, Musée du Québec, Quebec City, and National Gallery of Canada, Ottawa

**1968**

*Ten Quebec Painters,* Montreal and Quebec City

**1971**

Illustrations for the art book *Where Nests the Water Hen* by Gabrielle Roy

**1974**

Retrospective, organized by the Quebec Ministry of Cultural Affairs, Moscow, Leningrad, Prague, Antwerp, and Paris

*The Nativity* printed as a Christmas postage stamp by Canada Post

**1976**

*The Four Seasons,* Galerie Gilles Corbeil, Montreal

Portrait of Clément Richard, Speaker of the National Assembly of Quebec

**1977**

Portrait of Governor General Jules Léger and Madame Léger

**1978**

Solo exhibition, Place des Arts, Montreal

**1979**

Portrait of Queen Elizabeth II and Prince Philip

**1980**

Solo exhibition, Mira Godard Gallery, Calgary

**1981**

Publication of *Jean Paul Lemieux retrouve Maria Chapdelaine,* deluxe numbered edition of 5,000 copies (Montreal: Stanké)

**1983**

Exhibition, Galerie Lacerte-Guimond, Sillery

**1984**

*Jean Paul Lemieux: His Canada,* National Postal Museum, Ottawa

Exhibition, Maison Bélanger-Girardin, Beauport

**1985**

Exhibition, Concordia Art Gallery, Montreal

**1987**

Exhibition, Villa Bagatelle, Sillery

**1988**

Commemorative print *At Twilight* for the 50th anniversary of the publication of *Menaud, maître-draveur* by Félix-Antoine Savard

**1992**

*Jean Paul Lemieux,* Musée du Quebec, Quebec City

**1996**

*Children and Jean Paul Lemieux,* Musée des enfants de Laval – Maison des arts de Laval

**1998**

*An Island,* Centre d'exposition de Baie-Saint-Paul

# Suggestions for further reading


Brulotte, Gaëtan. *L'univers de Jean Paul Lemieux*. With a foreword by Anne Hébert. Saint-Laurent, Quebec: Fides, 1996.

Carani, Marie. *Jean Paul Lemieux*. Quebec City: Musée du Québec, 1992.

Harper, J. Russell. *Painting in Canada: A History*. 2nd ed. Toronto: University of Toronto Press, 1977.

Musée des beaux-arts de Montréal. *Jean Paul Lemieux*. Montreal: Simpson Press, 1967.

Quebec, Ministry of Cultural Affairs. *Jean Paul Lemieux: Moscow, Leningrad, Prague, Antwerp, Paris*. Quebec City, 1974.

Robert, Guy. *Jean Paul Lemieux ou la Poétique de la souvenance*. Quebec City: Garneau, 1968.

Robert, Guy. *Lemieux*. Translated by John David Allan. Toronto: Gage, 1978. Originally published as *Lemieux* (Montreal: Stanké, 1975).